RECIPES FROM

Amelia Now

The quarterly magazine of

Amelia Island, Florida,

compiled by

Helen Gordon Litrico

First Printing 1992
Second Printing 1999
Third Printing 2007

Copyright © 2007 by Helen Litrico

ISBN 13: 978-0-9677419-8-7
ISBN 10: 0-9677419-8-X

Lexington Ventures Publishing
1894 So. 14th Street, Suite 4
Fernandina Beach, FL 32034

Printed through InterPress, Ltd.
143 Lobelia Road
St. Augustine, FL 32086

#25, 6/F Metro Center
32 Lam Hing Street
Kowloon Bay, Kowloon
Hong Kong

Cover Photo by Gino Litrico

Printed in China

FOREWORD

My qualification for publishing this cookbook is that I am a good eater - not a good cook. In fact, I was graduated from college and launched into an advertising career before I knew how to cook anything more than coffee, toast, bacon and scrambled eggs. While I set out to memorize *The Joy of Cooking* in my twenties, I really didn't make much progress in the kitchen until I married Gino Litrico.

Here he was - not just an Italian but an Italian from Fernandina Beach, Florida! He loved good food - especially seafood - and he had a little knowledge and a lot of flair as to its preparation. I had never been very big on eating seafood, probably because I grew up hundreds of miles from the coast, and the seafood we had every Friday wasn't exactly fresh. This book, therefore, started out in the early 1970s as a primer for cooking seafood, as I was learning the hard way.

Next, I wanted to put into writing the wonderful dishes prepared by my mother-in-law, Joanna Litrico. She is a superb cook who never had a written recipe, never measured anything, and who had no daughter to whom she could pass down her secrets. By a process of observing, guessing and testing and re-testing, I have come pretty close to matching her dishes. (Forgive the tedious detail. It is her technique that makes the difference.)

Amelia Now came into being in the summer of 1975, and I introduced recipes into the format with the fall 1977 issue. The response was quite favorable, so I began begging all of my friends for family recipes or original recipes or original adaptations of established recipes. I credited the source of previously printed recipes such as those in local cookbooks. (I highly recommend to you *Centre Street Cookery, More Smorgasbord Secrets* and *From the Recipe Files of Brett* as well as *Southern Seafood Classics,* the official cookbook of the Southeastern Fisheries Association.)

When I was ready to print the *Amelia Now* cookbook, I decided to include some of my old standbys just for convenience. Like the good meatloaf I rarely get to fix because Gino considers it "depression fare," and the pecan pie that works better because of the one tablespoon of flour, and the biscuits I cook about once every seven years according to my son's account.

We hope you discover some new favorite here or maybe an old favorite you may have forgotten. Join us in thanking all of the good cooks who generously shared their recipes with us.

Helen Gordon Litrico

TABLE OF CONTENTS

Appetizers

CHEESE WAFERS
FROM: Grace Miller

1 stick oleo
1/2 lb. grated cheese
1 cup sifted flour
1/2 tsp. salt
Dash red pepper

Let oleo and cheese come to room temperature. Mix well. Mix with other ingredients. Shape into several long rolls about as big around as a quarter. Fold in wax paper and chill. Slice a scant 1/4 inch thick to bake. Make ahead and freeze if desired. Place on greased cookie sheet and bake at 325 degrees for about 15 minutes. Watch closely so they don't burn. Recipe can be doubled.

DEVILED CRAB BALLS
FROM: Karen Weihs

2 TBLS. butter
2 TBLS. minced onion & green pepper
2-1/2 TBLS. flour
1/2 cup milk
1/2 tsp. salt & dry mustard
4 drops Tabasco
1 cup crabmeat
Flour
1 beaten egg
Bread crumbs

Melt butter, saute onion and pepper. Add flour and cook a minute. Then stir in milk. Cook until thick. Blend in salt, mustard, Tabasco and crab. Chill and roll in balls, then roll in flour. Dip in egg and roll in crumbs. Brown. Drain on paper towels.

MARINATED SHRIMP
FROM: Karen Weihs

This is good for finger food using picks.
2-1/2 lbs. shrimp
1/2 cup celery tops
1/4 cup mixed pickling spices
3-1/2 tsps. salt
2 cups sliced onions
1-1/4 cups salad oil
3/4 cup white vinegar
2-1/2 TBLS. capers & juice
2-1/2 tsps. celery seed
1-1/2 tsps. salt
Dash Tabasco

In large pot of water, boil shrimp, celery tops, pickling spices and 3-1/2 tsps. salt for five minutes. Then drain, cool and peel. Alternate shrimp and sliced onions in a large bowl. Make marinade of last six ingredients and pour over shrimp and onions. Let stand in refrigerator for 24 to 48 hours. Remove from liquid and serve.

CHAFING DISH CRAB DIP
FROM: Karen Weihs

1 lb. crab meat
1 pint sour cream
1 large size cream cheese
3 TBLS. sherry
Dash red pepper
1/2 cup grated sharp cheese

Blend sour cream and cream cheese. Add all other ingredients and put in chafing dish over low heat. Sprinkle grated cheese on top. Add parsley for color.

8

SHRIMP DIP
FROM: Anne Coonrod

1 lb. small cooked shrimp, peeled and deveined
1 large pkg. cream cheese
2 TBLS. onion, minced
8 oz. sour cream
1/2 TBL. horseradish
2 TBLS. catsup
Salt to taste
1/2 TBL. lemon juice

Chop onion in food processor, drop in other ingredients except shrimp and mix. Add shrimp and chop until desired consistency. Serve with crackers or chips.

SHRIMP-ARTICHOKE SPREAD
FROM: Mrs. Pat Lee

14-1/2 oz. can artichoke hearts, drained and minced
1 cup mayonnaise
1 cup grated Parmesan cheese
1 small onion, grated
1 tsp. lemon juice
1 garlic clove, crushed
1 6-1/2 oz. can shrimp, chopped fine
1 tsp. tabasco or hot sauce
Salt and pepper
Dash Worcestershire

Mix well and put in ramekin. Bake at 350 degrees about 20 minutes or until bubbly. Serve hot with crackers. (Can substitute crab for shrimp.)

ARTICHOKE SPREAD
FROM: Scott Neal

Drain a 14 oz. can of artichoke hearts and mash. Combine with one cup Hellman's mayonnaise and 1/2 cup grated Parmesan cheese. Bake in greased pan in 350 degree oven for about 20 minutes or until brown.

SALMON SPREAD
FROM: DeWayne Meeks

To reduce our fat intake, we substituted drained yogurt cheese (about 6 oz.) for the cream cheese and 2 TBLS. of undrained non-fat yogurt for the sour cream. And we like the touch of curry.

1 small can salmon (6-1/2 oz. to 7-1/2 oz.)
1 pkg. (8 oz.) cream cheese
1/2 cup finely chopped green onions (about 5 small ones)
1/4 cup finely chopped celery (1 stalk)
1/4 cup finely chopped green pepper (about 1/3 of a large one)
2 TBLS. sour cream
1 TBL. lemon juice
1/8 tsp. black pepper
Dash of salt
1/4 cup finely chopped fresh parsley
1/2 to 1 tsp. curry powder (optional)

Blend all ingredients until well mixed. Refrigerate until ready to serve on your favorite cracker. Makes approximately 1-1/2 cups of spread.

KATIE HOOVER'S DIP
FROM: Claire Morgan

To reduce fat intake, we also tried this recipe substituting 1 cup no-fat yogurt in place of the sour cream and mayonnaise and it was still quite good.

1 can white shoe-peg corn
1 cup sour cream
1/2 cup mayonnaise
1/2 cup sharp cheddar cheese, grated
1/4 cup Parmesan cheese
1 TBL. grated onion

Drain the canned corn and mix with other ingredients. Chill.

GUACAMOLE DIP
FROM: Nan Sands

2 avocados (1 cup mashed)
1 TBL. lemon juice
1 TBL. grated onion
1 tsp. salt
1/4 tsp. chili powder

Combine 1 cup mashed, ripe avocado with rest of ingredients.
Spread top with 1/3 cup mayonnaise, sealing edges of bowl.
Chill. Stir in mayonnaise before serving. Serve with fresh
vegetable sticks or Fritos.

BLACK-EYED PEA PINWHEELS
FROM: Pat Lee

1 15-oz. can black-eyed peas, drained
1/4 cup margarine
1/4 tsp. seasoned salt
2 dashes hot sauce
Dash garlic powder
6 oz. Neufchatel cheese, softened (this is the lower cholesterol
cream cheese)
1 10-oz. pkg. 6" by 4" lean ham slices*
10 green onions, cut into 6" lengths**

Combine black-eyed peas, margarine, seasoned salt, hot sauce
and garlic powder in saucepan; bring to a boil. Reduce heat,
simmer uncovered 15 minutes, stirring occasionally. Remove
from heat, let mixture cool. Position knife blade in food
processor; add black-eyed pea mixture and cheese. Process 3
to 5 seconds. Scrape down sides of bowl. Process an
additional 5 seconds or until mixture is smoothly blended.
Spread about 3 tablespoons of pea mixture on each slice of
ham; place a strip of green onion on long edge of ham slices.
Roll up ham slice, chill. To serve, cut each roll into 1/2 " slices
and arrange pinwheels on plate. Makes about 6-1/2 dozen.

*Only the Lyke-It-Lean package has 10 thin slices.
**Since some people can't digest raw onions or green onions,
substitute the extra long canned asparagus cut to 6" or lightly
cook fresh asparagus if you find nice thin stalks.

SPINACH BALLS
FROM: Mrs. Edith Shurley

2 pkgs. frozen chopped spinach
2 large white onions, chopped
6 eggs, beaten 'til frothy
Worcestershire, several dashes
Salt (just a teeny bit)
1 pkg. Pepperidge Farms herb-flavored dressing
1 stick butter, melted
1 3-oz. box grated Parmesan

Cook spinach according to directions and drain 'til dry. (Getting it quite dry is the secret of success.) Combine with other ingredients. Mix well and chill well for easier handling. Shape into balls (about an inch across) and bake in a 350 degree oven about 12 minutes. Makes 60 balls. (These freeze well after shaping - just bake a little longer.)

PIZZA SQUARES
FROM: Helen Litrico

2 TBLS. chopped onion
1 TBL. butter
1 8-oz. can tomato sauce
1 cup grated Cheddar cheese
1 egg, beaten
1 cup pecans, chopped fine
1 cup unseasoned bread crumbs
1/8 tsp. Worcestershire sauce
1/2 tsp. salt

Brown onion in butter, add tomato sauce and simmer for 5 minutes. Mix with the cheese, egg, nuts, bread crumbs and Worcestershire. Pour into a buttered 8-inch baking pan and bake at 350 degrees for 25 minutes or until firm. Remove, cut into squares, roll in Parmesan cheese and serve with a toothpick in each square.

ANTIPASTO
FROM: Marge Fisher

1 quart catsup
1 quart small onions
1 quart cauliflower
1 quart mushrooms (stems & pieces)
1 quart canned string beans, cut up very fine
1 quart red & yellow peppers
1 quart dill pickles
1 quart vinegar
1 quart green stuffed olives
1 quart oil (Mazola or olive)
2 bunches celery
2 bunches carrots
2 cans oil sardines
2 TBLS. salt
1/2 lb. anchovies
1 lb. Tuna
1/2 cup sugar
1 hot pepper (optional)

Empty catsup, onions, mushrooms, string beans, vinegar, oil, salt and sugar into large cooking utensil. Cut cauliflower, carrots, peppers, pickles, olives, celery, sardines, anchovies and hot pepper into very small pieces (coarse veg. grinder). Separately cook cauliflower, carrots, peppers about half of regular cooking time. Drain and dump in the large cooking container. Use oil of sardines, tuna and anchovies. Bring all of the above to a boil, stirring occasionally. Boil 20 minutes. Put in thoroughly washed and sterilized canning jars. Makes 36-38 half pints.

PEPPERY CHEESE SQUARES
FROM: the late Sammy Mumford

4 large eggs, beaten
3 cups grated cheese (1/2 cheddar / 1/2 Monterey Jack)
1 4-oz. can green chiles, chopped
1/2 cup diced onion
1/2 cup chopped sweet red pepper

Preheat oven to 350 degrees. Mix all ingredients together. Pour into a greased 9" x 9" baking dish and bake for 1 hour.

13

HUMMUS
FROM: Joan Miller

1 TBL. Tahini (sesame seed paste)
1 TBL. olive oil
1 TBL. lemon juice
1 TBL. white wine Worcestershire
1 can garbanzo beans (chickpeas), reserving liquid
2 cloves garlic, minced
Liberal sprinkling of white pepper
Chopped parsley for garnish
Pita bread, toasted and broken into pieces

Combine first 7 ingredients in blender or food processor fitted
with metal blade. Process until smoothly blended. Chill. If mix
becomes too thick when chilled, add a little of the reserved
liquid. Serve garnished with parsley surrounded by pita bread.

WELL DRESSED SHRIMP
FROM: Mrs. Louis Bennett

Crush stuffing fine for this easy appetizer.
Stove Top stuffing
Raw shrimp, shelled with tails left on
Bacon cut in three pieces

Coat shrimp in dressing. Wrap bacon around each. Bake in
moderate 350 oven until bacon is crisp - about 17 minutes.

BAMBINI
FROM: Marie White

1 cup Ricotta cheese
1/2 cup grated Mozzarella
1/4 cup grated Parmesan
1 pkg. large flaky biscuits
20 very thin slices pepperoni

Combine cheeses in bowl. Half each biscuit, forming 20 pieces.
Shape each into an oval and press out flat. Place a slice of
pepperoni off center. Top with tablespoon of cheese mixture.
Moisten edges. Fold dough to edge. Pinch edges to seal.
Transfer to greased pan. Bake at 350 degrees for 20 minutes.

14

Soups & Gumbos

FROGMORE STEW
FROM: Karen Weihs

1/2 lb. unpeeled shrimp, per person
1/4 lb. hot Polish sausage, per person, cut in 2-inch pieces
1-1/2 pieces corn-on-the-cob, cut in half, per person
2 unpeeled new potatoes, per person
1 large onion, per person
1 stalk celery, chopped
2 TBLS. Old Bay seasonings
Sea Salt to taste
1 head of garlic
optional: crab claws or de-backed whole crab, not loose meat

In a large pot, bring water (twice the amount of ingredients) to a boil. Add onions, celery, garlic and seasonings and boil for 5 minutes. Add potatoes and boil for 5 minutes. Add corn and boil for 8 minutes. Add sausage and boil for 5 minutes. Add the shrimp and simmer for 2 minutes. Remove from heat, cover, and let stand 4-5 minutes. Serve in a large bowl with some of the liquid. Great for a crowd!

DEAN'S SEAFOOD BISQUE
FROM: Dr. Dean Briggs

1-1/2 small onions, chopped
1 stick butter
3 tsps. flour
1-1/2 cups milk
1/4 tsp. pepper
1 tsp. salt
1/4 cup sherry
1 cup white wine
1 can of tomatoes and juice
1 lb. crab
1 lb. small raw shrimp, cleaned and deveined
Cooked fish in pieces (opt.)

Saute onion in butter. Add flour and stir. Blend in milk, salt and pepper. Add sherry and white wine. (Taste to see if more salt needed.) Add tomatoes, shrimp, crab and optional leftover fish. Simmer 1-1/2 hours on low heat. Serves 6 to 8.

SHRIMP AND CRAB GUMBO
FROM: Helen Litrico

This is better made a day or two ahead and re-heated.
Freezes well.

6 slices bacon
1 large or 2 medium onions, chopped
2 cloves garlic, minced
3 1-lb. cans of tomatoes
4 cans consomme
1 carrot, diced
4 green onions, cut into rounds,including some of the green part.
1-1/2 lbs. shrimp, shelled and deveined
1 lb. crabmeat
1/2 tsp. cayenne pepper
2 or 3 bay leaves
1 tsp. salt
3 10-oz. pkgs. frozen sliced okra*
3 TBLS. chopped parsley
4 or more TBLS. flour
1/3 cup sherry

Saute bacon in skillet until crisp. Drain on paper towels, crumble into small pieces; set aside. In bacon fat, saute the regular onions (not green onions) and garlic until golden. Transfer to a very large pot and add tomatoes and consomme. Cover and bring to a boil. Add carrot and green onions and simmer for one hour. Add shrimp, crabmeat, cayenne pepper, salt and bay leaves. Reheat to boil again and add okra. Reduce to simmer and cook gently another hour, stirring occasionally, scraping bottom of pot. It's best to remove from heat, cool and refrigerate to blend flavors, then reheat or cook more the next day. Just before serving, add chopped parsley and sherry. Thicken with flour, if desired, worked to thin smooth paste with a little water. When thickened, add crumbled bacon. Serve over spoonful of cooked rice in big soup bowls. Makes 10 generous servings.

*May substitute fresh or canned

CRAB AND CORN CHOWDER
FROM: Ann Robas

This chowder can be enhanced by adding small cooked shrimp along with the crab. This is a very rich soup and can be adjusted to a lighter one by using more chicken broth and less cream. (We loved it rich all the way!)

1 stick butter or margarine
1 small onion cut in small pieces
1 small green pepper cut in small pieces
2 small potatoes, peeled and chopped in small pieces
2 celery stalks, cut in small pieces
1 tsp. salt
2 TBLS. all-purpose flour*
2 TBLS. sweet paprika
1 can chicken broth
1 can white corn, cream style**
1 can white shoe-peg whole kernel corn**
1 quart half-and-half
1/2 pint (8 oz.) whipping cream
1 pound claw crabmeat, picked over for shell

Using a 5-quart Dutch oven, melt butter or margarine over medium heat and add next five ingredients. Stirring frequently, cook for about 10 minutes. Add flour and paprika and cook another minute or two, stirring all the while. Pour in chicken broth and stir until thickened. Add corn and cream and stir often until hot. Pick over crabmeat carefully to avoid bits of shell. Add crabmeat to chowder. Serve hot. Makes about 10 to 12 cups.
*For thicker consistency, use 3 TBLS.
**Can substitute yellow corn

CHARLESTON SHE-CRAB SOUP
FROM: Karen Weihs

1/2 cup finely diced onions
1/2 cup finely diced celery
10 TBLS. butter
8 scant TBLS. flour
6 cups fish stock
pinch mace
1 tsp. Kosher or sea salt
1 tsp. white pepper
1 tsp. tomato paste
2 cups cream
2 TBLS. dry sherry
1-1/2 TBLS. brandy
10 oz. white crabmeat
1 tsp. crab roe

Saute onion and celery in butter until tender. Add flour, fish stock, mace, salt and pepper. Simmer for 15-20 minutes. Add cream, sherry and brandy and simmer for 2 more minutes. Add crabmeat and roe. Optional: add tomato paste for color. Serve in preheated soup cups with a dollop of whipped cream with an additional sprinkle of crab roe on top.

QUICK CRAB BISQUE
FROM: Nan Sands

1 can mushroom soup
1 can cream of asparagus soup
1-1/2 soup cans milk
1/2 lb. fresh crabmeat
1/4 cup sherry

Combine soups. Stir in milk and heat to about boiling. Add crab and heat. Add pat of butter. Just before serving, add sherry. Serves 4.

SHRIMP GUMBO
FROM: Karen Weihs

2 to 3 lbs. shrimp, boiled and shelled
3 to 4 lbs. okra, cut in medium pieces
1 large can tomato sauce
1 large can tomato paste
1 1-lb. can tomatoes
1 large onion, diced
4 sticks celery, cut up
1 bay leaf
Salt & pepper to taste
1 hot pepper and a bit of chopped parsley
1 quart broth of bouillon water

Saute celery and onion in oil. Add sauce and paste. Simmer 1/2 hour. Add broth. Saute okra in aluminum pot, taking care not to brown; add to first mixture. Add seasoning and simmer another half hour. Remove bay leaf. Add shrimp and simmer 15 minutes. Serve over rice. (May be frozen.)

SEAFOOD GUMBO
FROM: Willyne Blanchard

Must use cast iron pot:
1 cup Mazola
1 cup flour
2 large onions, chopped
3 stalks celery & leaves, chopped
2 green peppers, chopped
3 cloves garlic, minced
2 quarts water
Salt, red pepper & black pepper
File`
Lots of shrimp, crabmeat, oysters or one of the three.

Brown flour in Mazola to cocoa brown. Add onions, celery, green pepper, garlic and cook till soft. Add 2 quarts water and cook one hour. Add seafood. Cook till done. Don't overcook. Add about a tablespoon or two of file`. Remove from heat, if not to be served immediately. Reheat and serve over rice. Add more file` to taste.

ALLIGATOR CREEK GUMBO
FROM: the late Mills B. Lane

2 onions, chopped fine
1 bell pepper, chopped fine
1/4 cup cooking oil
1-1/2 lbs. okra, cut in rounds
3 8-oz. cans tomato sauce
1/4 tsp. Tabasco
1 tsp. Worcestershire sauce
1 tsp. salt
1/2 tsp. pepper
1/2 tsp. garlic (2 cloves chopped fine)
1 TBL. sugar
2 lbs. of shrimp, peeled and deveined
1 lb. claw crabmeat

Saute onions and bell pepper in oil until tender. Add okra and simmer until tender. Add all other ingredients except shrimp and crabmeat and simmer for 30 to 45 minutes. Stir in shrimp and simmer for 10 minutes. Stir in crabmeat and simmer for additional 10 minutes. Serve over cooked rice. Serves 8 and freezes well.

Variation: Edith Shurley adds 4 chopped fresh tomatoes when adding tomato sauce.

GINO'S FISH CHOWDER
FROM: Gino Litrico

With Gino, nothing is ever measured, and no dish is prepared the same every time. It depends upon what you happen to have on hand. Here's an estimate on the quantities from his latest adventure with the big pot: 3 or 4 lbs. of meaty fish backbones or heads if very fresh - grouper, drum, redfish, or cobia. (Can substitute plain fish meat.)

Pepper, salt, & Adolph's natural tenderizer
Water to cover
1/2 cup olive oil
6 or 7 cloves garlic, peeled & cracked
1 TBL. chopped parsley
4 1-lb. cans tomatoes
3 cups chopped onions, preferably Vidalia
1 cup chopped carrots
3 cups chopped celery
1 cup chopped bell pepper
1/2 cup combined fresh chopped parsley, thyme, basil and dill
6 cups chopped potatoes
1-1/2 cups okra
4 forkfuls of capers
Scant 1/4 cup rice vinegar
Dash hot sauce

Sprinkle salt, pepper and Adolph's on fish. Let sit 15-20 minutes. Put fish in pot with water to cover. Boil hard to separate meat and bones - may take a couple of hours. Cool enough to separate. Discard bones. Set aside fish meat and water. Start anew with a BIG pot and put in olive oil, garlic and parsley. Cook until garlic starts to brown. Remove garlic. Add tomatoes. Cook awhile, stirring occasionally. Add onions. Cook awhile. Add carrots, celery and bell pepper. Cook awhile. Add fresh herbs and potatoes. Cook awhile. Add the cooked fish and its water. Add okra. Cook awhile. Add capers, rice vinegar and hot sauce. Cook until potatoes are tender. Serves a crowd and freezes well.

SHRIMP AND SPAGHETTI SOUP
FROM: Pat Versaggi

This is a recipe handed down in the family of one of our shrimping pioneers, Salvatore Versaggi.

2 onions, chopped
1/4 cup olive oil*
1 or 2 cloves garlic
3 TBLS. tomato paste
2 bay leaves
Salt & pepper to taste
1 to 1-1/2 lbs. shrimp, cleaned and cut in pieces
1/2 lb. spaghetti**

Saute onion and garlic in olive oil. Add tomato paste and shrimp and stir together. Add 1 quart water and seasonings. Cook on low heat for 20-30 minutes. Add cooked spaghetti (broken into small pieces before cooking.) Serve with grated Parmesan cheese. 6 servings.
* original recipe called for 1/2 cup
**original recipe called for 1 lb.

DONAX ("Periwinkle") SOUP
FROM: Gino Litrico

2 quarts Donax
4 quarts water
Salt & pepper
2 large garlic cloves, mashed
Minced parsley
1 onion, finely chopped
2 large potatoes, diced

Wash Donax to remove sand. Combine all except potatoes and onion in big pot. Bring to boil, cover, cook about 20 minutes.* Strain off into another pot and discard shells. Add onion, potatoes, more minced parsley. Cover and cook until potatoes are done.

*At this point, can serve as plain broth, freeze for stock, or use as base for your own Clam Chowder-type recipe.

ANNE DUEY'S OYSTER STEW WITH GRITS
FROM: Centre Street Cookery

6 slices breakfast bacon
1 medium onion, chopped
1 pint oysters
1 quart milk
1 tsp. parsley (optional)
Salt and pepper to taste
2 cups boiling water
1 tsp. salt
3/4 cup grits
Butter

In heavy saucepot, fry bacon, remove and drain on paper towel.
Saute onion until clear, add oysters with liquid, heat until oyster
edges begin to curl, add milk. Heat on medium heat until
bubbles begin to appear at edges. Cut heat to simmer (do not
allow to boil); add salt, pepper and parsley, cook about 30
minutes. Just before serving, break up bacon into bits and
return to stew. Cook grits in boiling salty water. To serve, place
serving of grits in individual bowl, add dollop of butter and cover
with stew. Serve with oysterettes and tossed salad.

SEAFOOD GUMBO
FROM: The Shrimp Festival, Fernandina Beach

8 cans of tomatoes
1 tsp. sugar
1 cup olive oil
1 TBL. salt and 1 tsp. pepper
2 bay leaves
2 to 3 lbs. onions
1 cup uncooked rice
1 lb. okra, cut in chunks
1 lb. cooked peeled shrimp
1 pint crabmeat, picked over for shell
1 lb. flaked fish

Turn the onions translucent in the oil. Add tomatoes and
seasonings and simmer 2 hours. Add rice and okra and
continue simmering another hour. Close to serving time, add
shrimp, crabmeat and fish. Makes one gallon.

BLACK BEAN SOUP
FROM: Helen G. Litrico

1/2 lb. dried black beans
1-1/2 qts. water
Vegetable oil
1 large onion, chopped fine
4 cloves garlic, minced
1-1/2 or 2 green peppers, chopped fine
2 slices thick-sliced bacon, cut in half inch strips (optional)
1 ham bone
3 bay leaves, broken
Lawry's Seasoned Salt
Pepper
Pinch of red pepper
1 jigger sherry (or vinegar)
Cooked rice

Wash, drain and pick over beans. Soak in water overnight or
use quick method; boil 2 minutes, let stand 2 hours. Keep water
beans soaked in. Lightly saute onion, green pepper and garlic
in just enough oil to cover bottom of skillet and add to beans.
Add bacon, ham bone, bay leaves and seasonings. Cook
covered over very low heat, stirring occasionally, until beans are
tender and consistency is good. Takes several hours. Just
before serving, remove bay leaves and add sherry (or vinegar).
Serve over rice in shallow soup bowls. Serves 7-8.

VICHYSOISSE
FROM: Joe Talbird

4 TBLS. butter or margarine
5 medium mild white onions, chopped
3 stalks celery, chopped
6 large Idaho potatoes, peeled & chopped
2 sprigs parsley
6 cups chicken stock (or use canned)
Dash Worcestershire sauce
1 quart Half & Half
2 TBLS. finely chopped chives
Celery salt
Pepper

String celery if using outer stalks. Melt butter, cook onions and celery on low heat until limp. Add potatoes, parsley, stock and Worcestershire. Taste stock and add salt if needed. Cook until potatoes are tender. Chop in blender. Put in refrigerator container and add Half & Half, celery salt, pepper and chives. Stir and chill. Better made at least a day ahead. Freezes well. Makes a gallon.

COLD TOMATO-HERB SOUP
FROM: Sis Martin

1 bottle (32-oz.) Beef-a-mato juice
1 grated onion
1 cup chopped celery
1 green pepper, minced
1 tsp. salt
1 clove garlic
3 TBLS. lemon juice
2 TBLS. minced herbs of your choice*
1 peeled cucumber, cut into chunks
2 peeled ripe tomatoes, in wedges
1 dash of tabasco

Put juice in large bowl. Add onion, celery, green pepper, herbs, salt, garlic bud (latter split in half, pierced with toothpicks). Chill covered in refrigerator several hours or overnight. Just before service remove garlic and add remaining ingredients.

*Seems a lot at first but evens out when cucumber and tomatoes are added . We favor basil, oregano, dried parsley and thyme.

COLD MELON SOUP
FROM: Dee Laws

Combine 1 melon (cantaloupe or honeydew) cut-up, 1 cup yogurt, 1/2 cup whipping cream, a little honey or sugar. Whip in blender.

For a diet version, combine 1 melon cut-up and 1 cup diet yogurt in blender, adding skim Pet milk to right consistency. If fruit isn't sweet enough, add artificial sweetner.

Pasta

Before marrying into an Italian family, I thought that (1) the only kinds of pasta were spaghetti, noodles and macaroni; (2) that spaghetti sauce absolutely had to have meat in it; and (3) that you always put the salt in the water when you filled the pot so you wouldn't forget it. I've loved using a wide variety of pastas, and I've grown to love the meatless marinara sauce, but the salt business remains a mystery. When I ask any Italian why you must wait until the water is at a rolling boil before adding salt, the answer has something to do with "live water" and "dead water" and makes no sense whatsoever. However, they're pasta experts, so I wait for the rolling boil. (And I use a little metal disc that keeps the water from boiling over.)

MARINARA SAUCE
FROM: Helen Litrico

3 TBLS. olive oil or Mazola
3 cloves garlic, cracked
1 8 oz. can tomato sauce
2 14-1/2 oz. cans whole tomatoes (or a 28 oz. can of crushed tomatoes)
1 tsp. sugar
1 tsp. salt
3 or 4 broken fresh basil leaves (or a good sprinkling of dried)
Good sprinkling of oregano

Lightly brown garlic in oil. Discard garlic. Add tomato sauce, stir and cook a little. Add tomatoes, stir around, breaking up with spoon. Add sugar, salt, oregano and basil and cook, stirring frequently, until a good sauce consistency - about 30 minutes.

NONNIE'S MEATBALLS & SPAGHETTI
FROM: Mrs. Joanna Litrico

Meatballs:
1 lb. ground chuck
1/3 cup plain bread crumbs
3 sprigs cut up parsley
1 medium garlic, minced fine
2 eggs, beaten
1/4 cup finely grated Romano cheese
Dash salt and pepper
1 TBL. water or milk
Oil (Mazola preferred)
Sauce:
1 medium onion, sliced thin
1 6-oz. can tomato paste
1 8-oz. can tomato sauce
Salt and pepper
Water (equal to 2 tomato paste cans)
1/2 stick butter

Combine meat, parsley and garlic in one bowl. In second bowl combine bread crumbs, salt, pepper and grated cheese. Add in beaten eggs. Combine bread mixture into meat mixture. Mix well by hand. Taste and add seasonings if necessary. Add a little water or milk and mix more. Dipping hands in water between times, shape meat balls, reserving a little loose meat for the sauce. (She shapes hers more cylindrical than round.) Heat about half inch of Mazola in skillet. (Sprinkle in a little salt to reduce sticking.) Over medium high heat, brown meatballs well on all sides. Drain off and strain oil, throwing away crumbs left in skillet. Put clear oil (about 3 TBLS.) back in skillet to make sauce. Over medium heat, saute onion until limp. Add reserved loose meat mixture and brown well. Add tomato paste, stir and brown. Add tomato sauce, stir and brown. Add salt and pepper. Stir and cook about 5 minutes, then add water equal to 2 tomato paste cans. Reduce heat and cook down, stirring occasionally, about 20 minutes. When sauce is good consistency, add meatballs and allow to cook about 5 minutes. Just before serving, remove meatballs, add half stick butter to sauce and stir till melted. To serve, place a little sauce on platter, then add cooked, drained spaghetti, then more sauce and mix in with 2 forks. Serve meatballs around edge of platter or in separate bowl.

SHRIMPBALLS & SPAGHETTI
FROM: Mrs. Joanna Litrico

This recipe is the same as for regular meatballs except instead
of using ground chuck, use 1-1/2 lbs. raw shrimp, shelled,
deveined and chopped very fine or ground up, and increase the
amount of bread crumbs to 1 cup.

LASAGNA
FROM: Helen Litrico

1/2 lb. lasagna noodles
1 TBL. vegetable oil
2 TBLS. butter
1/2 cup chopped onion
1 clove garlic, chopped
1 lb. ground beef
1 6-oz. can tomato paste
1 28-oz. can tomatoes
1 tsp. salt
1/8 tsp. pepper
1/4 tsp. dried basil
1/4 tsp. dried oregano
3/4 lb. ricotta
1 egg, beaten
1/2 lb. mozzarella cheese, cut in thin strips
Parmesan cheese

Bring large pot of water to rolling boil, add salt and vegetable oil
to prevent sticking. Slide in 9 or 10 lasagna strips carefully.
Cook about 12 minutes. Drain, rinse with hot water. Melt butter
in large skillet; add onion and garlic and cook slowly for 5
minutes. Add ground beef and cook, stirring, until it loses red
color. Stir in tomato paste, cook briefly. Add tomatoes and
break up with sharp spoon. Add salt, pepper, basil and
oregano. Cook over low heat, stirring occasionally, about 30
minutes. Mix beaten egg in with ricotta. Butter a 13" x 9"
shallow baking pan. Place one-fourth of meat sauce in bottom,
then layer a third of the lasagna noodles, a third of ricotta and a
third of mozzarella. Repeat layers, ending with meat sauce on
top. Sprinkle with Parmesan cheese. Bake at 350 degrees for
35 to 40 minutes. Freezes well. Serves 8.

FRESH MARINARA SAUCE
FROM: Helen Litrico

4 TBLS. olive oil
8 or 9 garlic cloves
9 fresh tomatoes
1 15-oz. can tomato sauce
2 tsps. salt
1 tsp. sugar
Sprinkle of black pepper
1 tsp. dried oregano
9 basil leaves or 1 tsp. dried basil

Plunge tomatoes into boiling water to loosen skin. Remove skin. Put 7 tomatoes (in several batches) in blender or food processor and chop fine. Cut other 2 up in small pieces so there will be some texture in the sauce. Heat olive oil in skillet. Peel and crack garlic. Put garlic in oil and cook over medium heat until they start to brown. Remove from oil. Add to oil the tomatoes, tomato sauce and seasonings. Cook over medium heat about 2 hours. Cool, portion in containers and freeze.

(We get whole boxes of tomatoes, especially in May and August, at the Jacksonville Farmer's Market and cook a batch every night for a week.)

AMERICAN SPAGHETTI SAUCE
FROM: Helen Litrico

This recipe came from a restaurant via a former roommate, Barbara Stubbs.

3 lbs. ground chuck
2 stalks celery, chopped fine
5 bell peppers, chopped fine
5 medium onions, chopped fine
6 or 7 cloves garlic, minced
6 small cans tomato paste
3 bay leaves, broken
1/4 tsp. thyme
3 or 4 small cans mushrooms
3 tsps. salt
1-1/2 tsps. sugar
2 TBLS. Worcestershire sauce
1/2 tsp. each cinnamon, allspice, ground cloves
vinegar to taste

Cook vegetables in barely enough water to cover. When vegetables are tender, add meat and stir while cooking. When meat browns, add tomato paste, mushrooms and seasonings. Simmer about 3 hours, covered. Add a little water if sticking. Serves 18 - 20 and freezes well.

FISH SAUCE WITH SPAGHETTI
FROM: Mrs. Joanna Litrico

4 small whiting, absolutely fresh
(can substitute spot, trout or any mild fish)
2 TBLS. vegetable or olive oil
2 large cloves garlic
4 sprigs parsley, cut up
2 medium tomatoes, skinned (or 2 or 3 canned with a little juice)
1 cup water
1/2 tsp. salt
Dash pepper
3/4 lb. linguine or spaghetti

Wash the cleaned fish. Sprinkle salt liberally, inside and out, and set aside. (This firms the meat, though salt will be washed off later.) Mash garlic, put in oil over medium heat. After garlic cooks 2 or 3 minutes, add parsley. When garlic browns on edges, add tomatoes. Stir and mash tomatoes while cooking, about 10 minutes. Remove whole garlic. Add 1 cup water, cover and cook over low heat. When sauce begins to boil, wash salt off fish and add to sauce. Sprinkle salt and pepper. Cook about 20 minutes while cooking linguine or spaghetti. Remove fish to one plate. Put drained spaghetti in shallow soup bowls, pour sauce over spaghetti. Serve with fresh grated Romano cheese. Serves 4.

FISH-TOMATO SAUCE FOR SPAGHETTI
FROM: Mrs. Joanna Litrico

Mrs. Litrico's secret of a better-tasting sauce is adding one ingredient at a time, stirring well and cooking awhile before adding the next ingredient. For the 20-oz. of water in this recipe, we use the can measurings so you can scrape all the goody out of the cans.

4 steaks or chunks cut crosswise of fish, preferably flounder
(Good substitutes are drum, grouper, snapper and cobia)
Vegetable oil
1 medium onion, sliced thin and cut in halves
1 or 2 garlic cloves, cracked by pressing with heel of hand
1 6-oz. can tomato paste
Water (Tomato paste can twice, sauce can once)
1 8-oz. can tomato sauce
Salt and pepper (very little)
Fresh basil leaves (optional)

Wash fish and pat dry with paper towel. Sprinkle with a little salt. Over high heat, saute steaks in hot oil about a quarter-inch deep; cook until lightly browned on both sides, not totally cooked. Remove fish and set aside. Lift out any fish bits with slotted spoon, and pour off all oil except about 2 TBLS. Over low heat, saute onions and garlic in remaining oil, stirring constantly until brown. Stir in tomato paste, mix well and cook a few minutes. Add half of a paste can of water, mix well and stir a few minutes. Then stir in tomato sauce, mix well and cook a few minutes. Then add water again - 1-1/2 paste cans, 1 sauce can. When boiling well, add fish to sauce, cover and cook over very low heat until sauce thickens, about 20-22 minutes. Cook and drain spaghetti. Lift fish out of sauce and serve on a separate platter. Mix sauce with spaghetti. Serves 4.

SQUID SAUCE
FROM: Gino Litrico

Oil (Mazola)
6 cloves garlic, mashed
Handful parsley, chopped
1 medium onion, chopped
1 6-oz. can tomato paste*
1 8-oz. can tomato sauce*
4 1-lb. cans tomatoes
2 tsps. salt
1/2 tsp. red pepper
2 tsps. capers
3 lbs. cleaned, cut-up squid
1 lb. twists or other pasta
Parmesan cheese

Cover bottom of heavy pot with oil and heat. Saute garlic.
When edges start to turn brown, add parsley and saute. Add
tomato paste, stir and slightly brown. Add tomato sauce, stir
and cook a little. Crush tomatoes in blender and add with salt
and red pepper. Stir well. Cook covered over low heat, stirring
occasionally to keep from sticking, about 4-5 hours until it has a
good sauce consistency. Add capers and squid and cook 30-45
minutes more. Serve in soup bowls mixed with cooked, well
drained pasta. Sprinkle with Parmesan cheese. Serves 12-14.

*To get sauce consistency in less cooking time, double amount
of tomato paste and tomato sauce.

SQUID SAUCE FOR LINGUINE
FROM: Gino Litrico

With slight variations, this basic recipe is good with scallops, crabmeat or shrimp. With shrimp, for instance, we tone down the herbs and sometimes add sliced ripe olives and quartered artichoke hearts.

Olive oil
2 cloves garlic, cut in chunks
Chopped fresh parsley, dill and basil to taste.
(Make basil the largest proportion)
1 fresh tomato, chopped
1/3 cup fresh V-8 juice (optional)
7 to 8 oz. squid, cleaned and cut into small pieces
Black pepper
1/3 cup white wine
Slightly less than 1/2 lb. broken up linguine.
Grated Parmesan and Romano cheese

Heat oil in skillet. Quickly saute garlic chunks and add fresh herbs. Then add tomato and stir. (If tomato doesn't produce much liquid, add about 1/3 cup fresh V-8 juice or water.) Turn skillet low and cook linguine. When it's al dente, drain linguine and finish sauce. Add squid and white wine, sprinkle on pepper and cook briefly. Mix well with linguine and sprinkle grated cheese over top. Serves 2.

SHRIMP VEGETABLE PASTA
FROM: Rosalie Versaggi

1 pkg. frozen green peas
1 pkg. frozen broccoli, cauliflower and carrots
4 TBLS. butter
2 TBLS. olive oil
1 small onion, chopped
1 clove garlic, minced
1/2 cup chopped bell pepper
2 lbs. shrimp, cleaned, shelled and deveined
1 tsp. Italian seasoning
1/2 tsp. dry mustard
1/2 tsp. basil
Chopped parsley
2 green onions, sliced thin
1 can chicken broth or 2 cups shrimp broth*
1 TBL. cornstarch
12 oz. cooked linguine
Parmesan cheese

Cook green peas, drain and set aside. Place mixed broccoli, cauliflower and carrots in boiling salted water and boil until barely tender - not more than 3 minutes. Cut shrimp in half if large; sprinkle with pepper. In large deep skillet, melt butter and add olive oil and saute onion, garlic and green pepper. Add shrimp to skillet and add seasonings, parsley and green onions. Stir and cook until shrimp turn pink. Dissolve cornstarch in chicken broth or shrimp broth, add to skillet mixture and cook until thickened. Taste and add salt, if necessary. In large pot in which linguine cooked, combine skillet mixture, vegetables and cooked linguine. Toss with about 5 TBLS. Parmesan cheese. Makes 8 servings.

*Make shrimp broth by putting shells in large pan of salted water, cook about 15 minutes and then let shells sit in the water.

SHRIMP CRAB TOPPING
FROM: Joe Talbird

1 box spinach noodles (or other pasta)
2 Stouffer's Welsh Rarebits, frozen
1/2 stick butter
4 stalks celery, chopped fine
1 medium onion, chopped fine
2 cloves garlic, chopped fine
1-1/2 lbs. shrimp, shelled and deveined
1 lb. claw crabmeat
Juice of 1 lemon

Cook noodles and rarebits according to package directions while making topping. Melt butter. Saute celery, onion and garlic lightly. Saute shrimp in with vegetables until pink. Add crabmeat, sprinkle lemon juice over and stir to heat through. Blend rarebit and seafood mixture and mound on top of well drained noodles on platter. Serves 8 amply.

CAULIFLOWER SAUCE FOR PASTA
FROM: Mrs. Joanna Litrico

Preferred pasta is the smallest elbow macaroni or small shells.

1/2 head cauliflower
2 TBLS. olive oil
1 small or 1/2 medium onion, chopped
1 clove garlic, minced
2 TBLS. ragu (regular marinara sauce)
Salt and pepper
Romano cheese

Trim cauliflower. Bring large pot of water to boil, add salt, then add cauliflower. Cook till tender. Remove cauliflower with slotted spoon and drain, keeping same water for cooking pasta. While cooking pasta, heat oil in skillet, add onions and garlic and cook until limp. Add ragu and mix well. Then add drained cauliflower and mash into little pieces in the sauce. Add salt and pepper. Drain pasta and mix with cauliflower sauce. Sprinkle Romano cheese on top.

HOMEMADE NOODLES
FROM: Mrs. Paula Spinelli

It's better if two people work at this - one to turn the machine and one to catch noodle dough.

2 lbs. all-purpose flour
6 eggs
3/4 cup skim milk
1/2 tsp. salt
(If use only 1 lb. flour, use 4 eggs.)

Spread flour on table and clear a well in center. Drop eggs in center. Add salt. Beat eggs with fork. Circle around well of flour, adding a little each time. When mixture gets dry, add milk a little at a time. Then knead by hand, working in last of flour. Form into ball and pour last of milk into center. Work in by kneading by hand. Knead a few minutes and shape into a long tube. Slice into about 1-inch pieces and flatten with hand. Flour slightly. Put in machine at #1 (largest space). Roll through all pieces. Roll through again. Change machine to #2. Roll through once. Change to #3. Roll through once. Move to #5. Roll through once. Lay out on floured table. Then move handle to cutter you want (noodles). As noodles come out, catch in hand and spread out to dry, separating and sprinkling with flour to keep from sticking. Leave spread out at least one hour.

Shrimp

Since Fernandina Beach, Florida, is the birthplace of the modern shrimping industry, it's only natural that *Amelia Now* should feature shrimp recipes often. The Florida East Coast shrimp is said to be the "sweetest" in the world because of its lower iodine content. (There's an old saw about having to throw an Alka-Seltzer in the water for boiling Key West shrimp to make them palatable. This trick was discovered quite by accident by a shrimper with a hangover.)

Much of the pleasure of eating shrimp in Fernandina comes from the freshness of the product. Local residents and restaurants joy in serving fresh shrimp from the local boats. When the shrimp are plentiful, they stock up to freeze them right away in containers covered with water. Then, they have shrimp in mint condition, though frozen, to serve at those times when Northeasters keep the boats tied up at the docks for days. Best to thaw by running cold tap water on them.

BOILED SHRIMP
FROM: Gino Litrico

Everybody on the island has his or her own way of boiling shrimp, ranging from simply cooking them in beer laced with Zatarain's Crab Boil to very spicy concoctions. The most important thing is not to overcook. Cooked plain or fancy, the shrimp are usually served in the shells in Fernandina, so each eater peels his own.

Here's Gino's recipe:

5 lbs. fresh shrimp in shells
Water to cover
1 to 1-1/2 oz. vinegar
Juice of one lemon
2 to 3 TBLS. salt
4 to 5 bay leaves
1 TBL. whole coriander
Dash red pepper
1 tsp. celery seed
2 to 4 whole cloves

Wash shrimp thoroughly. Combine all ingredients in large pot (avoid aluminum) and cover. When it starts to steam, start timing. In four minutes, peek and see if shrimp meat is starting to pull away from the shell. Then remove from heat, remove cover and let cool in spicy water. Serve in shells with lemon butter or a bland sauce which doesn't overpower the shrimp. To about 3 heaping tablespoons of mayonnaise, Gino adds a little ketchup, mustard, lemon juice, dash of Worcestershire sauce and a dash of hot sauce. Mix well.

In Fernandina fashion, cover the table with newspapers, mound the drained shrimp (still in the shell) in the center, add sauces and lemon wedges and let everybody dive in!

WATERLESS SHRIMP
FROM: Nancy Hines

Do this only with a small quantity of definitely fresh shrimp. When cooking starts, stir frequently so shrimp cooks evenly. Be sure meat starts pulling away from shell before removing from heat. (We undercooked on first try.) Nancy feels shrimp stays more tender and juicy cooked by this recipe from Mobile.

Place shrimp in a pot with *no* water. Sprinkle with lemon juice if desired and cook covered about three minutes - or until shrimp are pink and juicy. Remove from heat, add salt, cover again. Let stand about 20 minutes before serving.

TANGY THICK SHRIMP SAUCE
FROM: DeWayne Meeks

1 cup Heinz Ketchup (hot)
2 TBLS. mayonnaise
1-1/2 TBLS. French's mustard
1/2 tsp. Lawry's seasoned salt
1/2 tsp. garlic powder
1/2 tsp. celery salt
3/4 tsp. onion powder
Pinch of cayenne pepper
1 TBL. hot sauce if desired

DeWayne uses Mexi-Pep as his preferred hot sauce. Blend all ingredients with spoon until smooth. Serves 4.

FRIED SHRIMP
FROM: Traditional

Every cook on the island has his or her own little touch, but here is the basic recipe:

1 lb. large fresh shrimp
1 egg, beaten
1 TBL. water
1 tsp. salt
2/3 cup breading (usually plain bread crumbs or Bisquick or cracker meal with 2 TBLS. flour added)
Hot cooking oil, preferably peanut oil

Peel shrimp, keeping tail, devein and wash well. Drain. Combine beaten egg, water and salt. Dip each shrimp into egg mix, then roll in breading and drop into deep fryer of hot oil. Cook just 2 or 3 minutes. Serves 4.

Pancake Batter: Add 1 tsp. salt to leftover pancake batter. Dip in shrimp and shake off excess. Fry in hot oil. Browns beautifully.

Beer Batter: Mix equal parts beer and flour. Let stand 3 hours before using to batter shrimp.

Lorraine Corbett's Batter: Mix equal parts of Bisquick, cornstarch and water. Maybe a little extra water to keep it nice and light.

Lynn Miller's Batter: Combine 1 cup flour, 1 beaten egg, 1 TBL. oil, pinch of baking soda and 3/4 to 1 cup beer. Mix slightly and let sit for at least one hour. Dip and fry in hot peanut oil. (Can roll in flour and then dip in batter.)

Lynn Miller's Other Batter: Combine half a cup of sour cream and 1 beaten egg. Combine equal parts of cracker meal, pancake mix, regular flour and bread crumbs. Dip shrimp in sour cream-egg mix, then in dry mix before frying.

BUTTERFLY SHRIMP
FROM: Pat Williams

2 lbs. raw large shrimp
1 cup beer
1 tsp. salt
2 eggs
2 TBLS. cooking oil
1/8 tsp. cayenne
1-1/4 cups all-purpose flour

Remove shell, leaving tails intact. Slit shrimp deeply down back without cutting all the way through and remove black vein. Wash well. Spread shrimp open on absorbent paper and cover with more paper. Keep cold until ready to fry. Combine beer, salt, eggs, oil and cayenne; gradually stir in flour. Let batter stand 5 minutes before using. Stir frequently during use. Dip shrimp one at a time into batter and drop into hot fat. Fry few at a time for 2 minutes or until lightly browned. Drain on absorbent paper. Sprinkle with salt and serve hot with lemon wedges. Serves 4 to 6.

BUTTERFLY SHRIMP
FROM: Marge Crawford

2 lbs. Royal Red shrimp*
2 eggs, separated
3/4 cups beer
1 TBL. olive oil
1 cup flour

Peel shrimp, leaving tails intact, devein and wipe dry. Slit shrimp down back without separating halves; press each shrimp flat to form a butterfly shape. Make a fritter batter of egg yolks beaten with beer, olive oil and sifted flour. Fold in stiffly beaten egg whites. Dip each shrimp in flour and then in the batter; fry in deep hot fat for 4 minutes or until golden brown. Drain shrimp on absorbent paper; serve with soy sauce and hot mustard. Yield 4-6 servings.
*These sweet tender shrimp are back on the market in Fernandina after an absence of three years.

BUTTERFLIED SHRIMP WITH SWEET & SOUR SAUCE
FROM: the late Mills B. Lane

A side benefit of this tasty dish is that the batter doesn't fall off during cooking; you can cool and re-bottle the oil.

2 lbs. raw jumbo shrimp
Baking soda
1 cup water
1 cup flour
2 heaping tsps. baking soda
Salt and pepper
Quart or more of Mazola (or peanut oil)

Peel shrimp, leaving tails on. With sharp knife, slice through back, not quite all the way through. Spread shrimp out flat and devein. Put shrimp in bowl, sprinkle baking soda over, mix together. Refrigerate a half hour to an hour. Then wash off soda and drain shrimp. Make batter of water, flour, baking soda, salt and pepper to taste. In deep skillet (big enough to hold at least a quart) heat oil to 375 degrees or more. Holding shrimp by the tail, dip into batter, shake off excess and drop into hot oil. (Do in batches of about 6 at a time.) Turn once or twice with spatula until golden brown. Drain on absorbent paper. Serve with sweet & sour sauce to 6.
Sauce: Heat a half cup of Dundee's orange marmalade. Add 2 tablespoons of red wine vinegar. Combine 1-1/2 teaspoons Colman's dry mustard with enough water to reach consistency of cream and add to marmalade/vinegar mixture. If you want mustard hotter, add pinch of sugar. (Measurements are tester's estimates. Mr. Lane just says "some".)

SPANISH FRIED SHRIMP
FROM: Dr. Humberto Lamas

In small saute pan, put 1/4 inch equal parts oil and vinegar. When this comes to a boil, add shrimp in shells. Sprinkle on salt and cracked pepper. When shells pull away from the meat, remove shrimp and serve with a big salad and some good bread.

BIG DADDY'S BATTER FOR FRIED SHRIMP
FROM: Gene Sanders

We used to keep this dry mix in the refrigerator at all times.

Mix well:
5 lbs. self-rising flour
1 lb. Hungry Jack Extra Light Pancake flour (blue box)
Salt and pepper to taste
McCormick Barbeque Spice - sprinkle liberally
McCormick Italian Seasoning - sprinkle liberally
Pinch of sage

Beat together well:
3 eggs (sometimes 4)
1 pint buttermilk

Dip shrimp in egg mix, then in dry mix. Fry in hot oil.

TEMPURA
FROM: Mrs. Matsu Ball

2 lbs. large fresh shrimp
1-1/8 cups all-purpose flour
1 egg
1 cup water
Cooking oil, preferably peanut oil

Shell shrimp, keeping tails, and devein. Slit underside of shrimp to flatten out. Wash and dry thoroughly. Prepare batter by beating egg and water, adding flour and mixing lightly. Two or three stirs should be enough even though some lumps remain. (Don't overmix!) Fill deep saucepan or deep fryer at least three-quarters full of cooking oil and heat until very hot. Dip shrimp one at a time into batter and drop into hot oil. Cook only a few at a time. Large bubbles form. When bubbles become small, tempura is done. (Overcooking will toughen.) Drain and serve hot with warm sauce.
Tempura Sauce:
Combine 1/2 cup soy sauce, 1/2 cup of fish stock or mild bouillon and 2 tsps. sugar. Optional pinch of Accent.

SHRIMP GRAVY
FROM: Traditional

2 TBLS. (or about 2 oz.) diced salt pork
1/2 cup minced onion
1/2 cup minced green pepper
1 garlic clove, minced
1-1/2 lbs. raw shrimp, shelled and cleaned
1 cup water
1/2 tsp. coloring (like Kitchen Bouquet)
Salt & pepper to taste
Dash Worcestershire
Pinch dried, crushed red pepper
Cooked rice

In skillet, cook salt pork over medium heat. Remove with slotted spoon to drain on paper. Pour off half of fat. In remaining fat cook onion and pepper till limp. Cut shrimp in small pieces if large. Add shrimp to vegetables and cook, stirring, until they turn bright pink and tender - about 3 minutes. Remove vegetables and shrimp to warm place. To fat in pan, add water and coloring. Bring to boil while stirring and simmer a couple of minutes. Season to taste with salt, pepper, Worcestershire and red pepper. Return pork, shrimp and vegetables to skillet to reheat briefly. Serve over cooked rice. Serves 4.

STEWED SHRIMP GRAVY
FROM: J. J. Van Goidtsnoven

Peel and devein 1 lb. small to medium shrimp. Add garlic powder, salt, pepper and Accent to shrimp and set aside. Fry about 6 to 8 slices of smoked bacon until crisp. Drain and crumble. Saute 1-1/2 cups chopped onion, 1 cup chopped celery and 1/4 cup chopped bell pepper until soft in the bacon drippings. Drain vegetables. Sprinkle shrimp with about 1/2 cup flour. Toss until "gooey". Add to vegetables with enough water to cover and add more garlic powder and Accent. Simmer until the consistency of gravy. Serve over rice. Serves 3.

SHRIMP GRAVY

FROM: Mrs. Betty Anderson

About 2 oz. white bacon (unsmoked salt pork), cut in cubes
1/2 cup green pepper, chopped fine
1/2 cup celery, chopped fine
2 lbs. raw shrimp, shelled, deveined and floured
1 env. Lipton's onion soup mix
Water (about 1 cup)
Pepper

Fry white bacon until golden brown. Remove. Pour off excess
fat. (If not enough fat rendered for sauteing, add little vegetable
oil.) Saute chopped celery and bell pepper. Remove. Add
floured shrimp and stir until lightly cooked. Add Lipton's onion
soup mix to the saute and add water to gravy consistency.
Return bacon, celery and bell pepper to shrimp. Add little
pepper. (No salt necessary.) Cook over lowest heat about 10
minutes to meld flavors. Serve over cooked rice to 6 people.

CAP'N ROBERT'S SHRIMP GRAVY

FROM: Joe Talbird

Fry a half pound of cut-up bacon. Remove. Add 2 large
chopped onions and 2 cups water to bacon drippings and cook
until onions are tender. Return bacon to sauce, cover and
simmer. Peel, devein and wash 2 dozen medium shrimp.
Prepare grits for 4. When close to done, place raw shrimp in
simmering grits. They'll quickly steam done. To serve, top the
shrimp-grits with bacon gravy.

SHRIMP PILAU
FROM: Mrs. Bea Lyons

2 lbs. raw shrimp
4 oz. white bacon (unsmoked salt pork)
1 large onion, chopped
2 cups water
Salt & pepper to taste
1 TBL. sugar
2 cups raw rice, washed

Shell, devein and wash shrimp. Drain and let dry. Cut white
bacon in small cubes and fry. Add chopped onion. Add shrimp
and stir a bit so barely starts cooking. Add 2 cups of water, salt
and pepper to taste, and stir. For darkening agent, burn 1 TBL.
sugar separately over hot fire, add a little water to it and pour
into shrimp mixture. Add 2 cups raw rice. Turn to medium heat
and let boil until water almost boils out. Turn very low until rice
gets done. (No lid.) About 5 servings.

SHRIMP PILAU
FROM: the late Mrs. M. L. Griffin

1/4 lb. white bacon (uncured salt pork), diced
2 large onions, chopped
1 cup raw rice
1-3/4 cups water
1 tsp. salt
1/4 tsp. pepper
1-1/2 lbs. raw shrimp, shelled
2 tsps. Kitchen Bouquet

Fry out white bacon. Brown onions. Add rice, water, shrimp
and seasoning. Let come to a hard boil. Cover and simmer
about 30 minutes. For best results, use a Teflon pot. Serves 6
to 8.

SHRIMP PILAU
FROM: Eloise Blue

1/4 cup cooking oil
1 lb. shrimp, peeled, deveined and cut in half (unless small)
Salt, pepper, paprika, flour
1 medium onion, chopped fine
1 cup celery, chopped fine
Half of medium bell pepper, chopped fine
1 tsp. Kitchen Bouquet (optional)
3 cups water
2 cups rice, washed
3 TBLS. butter or margarine

Spread shrimp on wax paper and season with salt, pepper, paprika. Sprinkle lightly with flour. Heat oil. Add onion, celery and bell pepper and cook down slowly. Add shrimp and cook until all light brown. If gravy isn't brown enough, add Kitchen Bouquet. Add 3 cups water, and when it comes to a boil, add raw rice. Turn to low. Add salt to taste. Let simmer until rice is done, about 20 minutes. At end, dot with butter and when it melts, toss rice with fork. Serves 4.

BAKED SHRIMP PILAU
FROM: Karen Weihs

This is a Charleston-style recipe, quite different from the local recipes starting with white bacon in a skillet. The editor finds this an easier way to arrive at a similar result.
1 cup raw rice
Small chopped onion
2 TBLS. margarine or butter
1 lb. raw shrimp, shelled and cleaned
1 can mushroom pieces and juice
1 bell pepper, chopped
1 large rib celery, chopped
2 chicken bouillon cubes
2 cups water
Season to taste (We use 2 tsps. salt and 3 dashes pepper)

Fry onion and rice in margarine or butter until light brown. Dissolve bouillon cubes in water. Put all ingredients in covered casserole and bake 1 hour at 350 degrees. Stir every 15 minutes.

GINA SPILLER'S SHRIMP PILAU
FROM: Vieni a Mangiare

*Vieni a Mangiare ("Come to Dinner") is a privately printed
cookbook of recipes of the Versaggi family. It is a delightful
compilation of both authentic Sicilian dishes and purely
imaginative originals.*

1/2 lb. white bacon, diced
2 medium onions, chopped
1 large can tomatoes
1 green pepper, chopped
10 whole cloves
1/2 tsp. thyme
2 lbs. shrimp, shelled and deveined
3 cups rice, washed 3 times
4 cups water
salt and pepper
1 datil pepper

Render diced bacon in heavy duty pot. Add chopped onions,
green pepper. When limp, add can of tomatoes, cloves, thyme,
datil pepper, salt and pepper. Cook until thick consistency. Add
shrimp and water and cook for 3 to 5 minutes. Add raw rice and
bring to a rolling boil. Cover and turn heat down very low. Cook
for 12 to 15 minutes. Stir and remove from heat. Allow to stand
an additional 30 minutes or until rice is done.

NOTE: Chicken, pork or ham pilau is made the same way
except chicken, pork or ham should be fried before adding to
tomato mixture. Also raw squid cut in bite size pieces may be
used instead of shrimp.

FRESH SHRIMP SAUTE
FROM: Gino Litrico

This basic recipe can be varied with your own choice of herbs:
1-1/2 lbs. shrimp, shelled, deveined and washed
2 TBLS. butter, melted
Splash of olive or vegetable oil
3 garlic cloves, mashed
1 chunk chopped fresh parsley
1 small chile pepper, minced (optional)
1/8 to 1/4 cup white wine or vermouth
1 TBL. flour
Minimum salt and pepper to taste

Heat butter and oil. Brown garlic, parsley and optional chile pepper. Add shrimp and stir couple of minutes until shrimp turn pink. Add wine and cook a minute. Add flour. Stir and coat shrimp. When evenly thickened, quickly remove from heat and sprinkle with salt and pepper. Serve over rice with a good white wine.
VARIATION: To avoid lumps in sauce, dust shrimp with flour prior to cooking instead of adding loose flour to sauce.

EASY SHRIMP SAUTE
FROM: Helen Litrico

1 lb. raw shrimp, shelled and deveined
Little over 1/3 cup Lea & Perrin's White Wine Worcestershire
3 TBLS. butter
Marinate shrimp in White Wine Worcestershire about 5 to 10 minutes, stirring several times to get all shrimp covered. No other seasoning is necessary. Saute briefly in butter. Make sauce by adding marinade to leftover butter and burn off alcohol.

SHRIMP AND HERBS
FROM: Gino Litrico

Mash 3 garlic cloves and brown in olive oil. Add dash of chevril, thyme, paprika, red pepper and parsley flakes. Stir. Dredge shrimp in flour, quickly brown in oil-herb mixture a minute. Add juice of lemon and white wine. Simmer 4 minutes. Sprinkle black pepper over.

50

GREEK SHRIMP
FROM: Lynn Miller

8 ripe tomatoes, peeled and diced
3 cloves garlic, chopped fine
1 small onion, chopped
3 TBLS. olive oil
1/4 tsp. oregano
1/4 tsp. rosemary
Salt and pepper to taste
2 dozen raw shrimp, peeled and deveined
Feta cheese

Saute tomatoes, garlic and onion in oil until tender. Add seasoning and simmer covered for one hour. Place 6 shrimp in each individual ramekin (4 in all) and cover with the sauce. Top with Feta cheese and bake in a 375 degree oven for 20 to 25 minutes. Serves 4. Serve with French bread.

BEIJING SHRIMP
FROM: Fran Kerr

1 cup chopped onion
1-1/2 cups chopped celery
1/2 cup (or a 2-1/2-oz. can) sliced mushrooms
1 14-oz. can bean sprouts, drained
1/2 cup chicken broth
1/4 cup soy sauce
2 TBLS. butter, melted
1/2 tsp. brown sugar
Salt & pepper to taste
2 lbs. medium shrimp, peeled and deveined
3 TBLS. water
3 TBLS. cornstarch

Saute onion and celery in butter until tender. Add all but water and cornstarch. Stir well. Simmer 5 minutes, stirring often. Combine water and cornstarch, stirring until smooth. Add to shrimp mixture. Cook over low heat until thick and bubbly. Serve over hot cooked rice or chow mein noodles. Serves 6-8. OPTIONAL: Can of drained pineapple chunks.

SHRIMP MULL
FROM: Mrs. Jimmie Salvador

1 lb. raw, peeled, deveined shrimp
3 oz. salt pork, chopped
1/2 cup chopped celery
1/2 cup chopped green pepper
1/2 medium onion, grated
1 clove garlic, minced
1-1/2 cups water
1 cup drained canned tomatoes, broken into pieces (or one cup fresh diced tomato)
1 cup uncooked rice
1/2 cup dry white wine
1 tsp. chopped parsley
1 tsp. Worcestershire sauce
1/2 tsp. salt
1 bay leaf
Pinch saffron, optional

Cut large shrimp in half. In a 3-quart saucepan, cook pork until crisp. Add celery, green pepper, onion and garlic; cook until vegetables are tender but not brown. Add remaining ingredients except shrimp. Cover and cook over low heat 18 to 20 minutes. Mix in shrimp, cover and continue cooking 10 to 12 minutes or until shrimp are tender. Serves 6 to 8.

SHRIMP KABOBS
FROM: Anne Coonrod

2 lbs. jumbo shrimp, peeled and deveined
Juice of one lemon
Italian dressing
Salt to taste

Combine lemon juice, Italian dressing and salt. Marinate shrimp for 1 to 2 hours. Alternate on skewer with cherry tomatoes, onion, mushrooms and green peppers. Grill for 5 to 10 minutes. Serve on a bed of yellow rice or rice pilaf.

HOT SHRIMP SALAD
FROM: Mrs. Jimmie Salvador

2 cups cooked, peeled, deveined shrimp, fresh or frozen
2 cups chopped celery
1/2 cup chopped green pepper
1/2 cup slivered almonds
1/2 cup mayonnaise or salad dressing
1/2 cup condensed cream of celery soup
1 jar (2 oz.) sliced pimientos
2 tsps. grated onion
2 tsps. lemon juice
1/2 tsp. salt
3 cups crushed potato chips
1/2 cup grated cheddar cheese

Thaw shrimp if frozen. Rinse shrimp thoroughly and drain. Cut large shrimp in half. Combine all ingredients except potato chips and cheese; mix well. Pour into a well-greased 2-quart baking dish or into 6 well-greased scallop shells or ramekins. Bake in moderate oven, 350 degrees, for 20 minutes. Combine potato chips and cheese; mix well. Sprinkle over shrimp mixture. Return to oven and continue cooking for 10 minutes or until thoroughly heated. Makes 6 to 8 servings.

GRILLED SHRIMP
FROM: Gino Litrico

Peel and devein shrimp. Drain. Dust with white and black pepper and granulated garlic. Cover the bottom of a skillet with olive oil, then add 1 teaspoon of jalapeno sauce and melt in 2 tablespoons of butter. Remove from heat and let cool. Put shrimp in oil-butter mixture and mix well. Marinate for 30 minutes or more. Grill on small mesh screen, using tongs and a spatula.

*Variation: Add curry and / or turmeric.

SHRIMP CREOLE
FROM: Willyne Blanchard

1 cup Mazola
1 cup flour
2 cups chopped onions
1 cup chopped celery
1/2 cup green pepper, chopped
2 cloves garlic, chopped
3 TBLS. tomato paste
2 TBLS. sugar
2 quarts water (approximately)
1/4 tsp. red pepper or more
1/2 tsp. black pepper or more
1 TBL. salt, more or less
1/4 tsp. thyme
2 bay leaves
3 lbs. raw shrimp, peeled and deveined
1 lemon, sliced
2 TBLS. parsley, chopped
3 green onions, chopped
4 cups cooked rice

In a cast iron pot, make a roux of the Mazola and flour. Brown slowly to a Hershey bar color brown. (Do not burn. If you try to hurry the roux, you may burn it and then you must start over.) To the roux, add chopped onions, celery, green pepper and garlic. Cook until all vegetables are soft. Add tomato paste that has been mixed with the sugar. Brown tomato paste in the roux for a few minutes, then add about 2 quarts of water, red pepper, black pepper, salt, thyme and bay leaves. Cook about an hour. Add shrimp. Cook half an hour. Just before serving, add the sliced lemon, parsley and chopped green onion. Serve on hot rice. Serves 6. Best if sauce is cooked a day or so ahead and stored in refrigerator without the shrimp. May be frozen.

GRILLED SHRIMP
FROM: Anne Coonrod

This is also good for fish - especially King Mackerel.

Allow half pound shrimp per person. Peel, leaving tail on, and devein. Marinate at least four hours in Seven Seas Italian Oil and Vinegar Dressing, salt and juice of half-lemon. Put on skewers* and cook on grill one to two minutes each side, turning once until pink on both sides. Do not overcook.
*If no skewers handy, use piece of screen.

SHRIMP ROCKEFELLER
FROM: Nancy Hines

1/2 lb. fresh spinach, washed, drained, dried in a towel
6 scallions or little onions
1/2 head of lettuce
1-1/2 stalks celery
1 clove garlic
1/2 cup chopped parsley

Chop all together   should be about 1 quart greens. Simmer together 10 minutes or less in the following:
1/2 cup butter
1 TBL. Worcestershire sauce
2 tsps. anchovy paste
1-1/2 tsps. salt (or less)
Dash of Tabasco

Add 1/2 cup soft bread crumbs to green mixture. Go easy on salt seasoning and taste before adding last 1/2 tsp. salt. Spread green mixture over 6 to 8 ramekins or scallop shells, depending on size. Cover with 2 lbs. shrimp, cooked, shelled and deveined. Make cream sauce of the following: 3 TBLS. butter, 1-1/2 cup milk*, 3 TBLS. flour, 3 TBLS. grated Parmesan cheese, 3/4 tsp. salt, pepper to taste. When thickened to right consistency, pour over shrimp and greens. Sprinkle with buttered crumbs and bake at 350 until sauce bubbles through. Serves 6 to 8.
*Can reduce milk and let some of liquid be sherry and/or water in which shrimp were boiled.

ETOUFFEE
FROM: Hon Versaggi and Peg Rentrop

1/2 stick butter or oleo
1 cup chopped celery
1 cup chopped onion
1/2 cup chopped parsley
1/2 cup chopped green onion
1 lb. cleaned raw crayfish or rock shrimp
1/2 cup water

In a heavy medium size pot (not black iron pot) cook onions and celery in butter till wilted, about 12-15 minutes. Add green onions and parsley and cook 6-8 minutes longer. Season with salt and pepper (or 1 tsp. "Tony Chachere" seasoning if available.) Add meat and cook 6-8 minutes more. Use no cover while cooking. When complete, cover to steam juices together. Use medium heat throughout. Add the water if needed for more gravy. Serve over rice. 4 servings.

VARIATIONS: Add one can of cream of shrimp soup when adding meat but add no water. K. Paul Prudhomme's seasoning is also good.

SHRIMP A LA MANALE
FROM: Louise Fishel

Line cake roll pan with foil. Place a layer of peeled shrimp in pan. In saucepan, bring to a boil:
1/2 lb. butter or oleo
1 or 2 TBLS. black pepper
1/2 tsp. garlic salt
2 tsps. Crab Boil

Pour over shrimp. Bake at 450 degrees for a few minutes. Good with a salad and French bread, which you dip into the sauce.

SHRIMP CURRY

FROM: Betty Collins

4 TBLS. butter
1 large onion, chopped fine
1/2 cup apple, chopped fine
1/2 cup celery, chopped fine
1 cup water or enough to cover veggies
3 lbs. shrimp, boiled and cleaned
2 TBLS. curry powder
1 pint cream
Salt and pepper to taste

Put butter in frying pan. Add onion, apple and celery. Simmer, add water. Let all simmer until tender and most of the liquid is cooked away. Stir seasonings into mixture. Add cream and shrimp. Cook gently until cream is reduced to sauce consistency. Serve with rice. Have small bowls of grated coconut, chutney, chopped almonds, raisins, chopped egg and pickle relish. Serves 8.

P.S. To reduce the fat intake, we cut out all butter, sprayed the pan with Pam, and let the veggies cook in the water. Then we replaced the cream with low-fat milk and added a teaspoon of arrowroot as a thickener. We also used just two lbs. of shrimp and cut them in half. Still tasted great.

SHRIMP CACCIATORE
FROM: Gino & Helen Litrico

This is adapted from a Minute Rice recipe. "Cacciatore" means "hunter". When you cook hunter-style, you vary the recipe according to what you have on hand.

2 TBLS. olive oil
1/2 cup chopped onion
1 garlic clove, minced
1/2 cup chopped celery
1/4 cup ripe olives, sliced
1/2 tsp. capers
1 lb. raw shrimp, shelled & deveined
1 can (14-1/2 oz.) whole tomatoes
1 can (8 oz.) tomato sauce
1/2 tsp. oregano leaves
1/2 tsp. dried basil
1 cup dry Minute Rice

Saute onion, garlic, celery, olives and capers in oil 4 or 5 minutes. Add shrimp and continute sauteeing until shrimp turn pink. Add tomatoes, tomato sauce and seasonings. Bring to a full boil. Stir in rice. Cover, remove from heat. Let stand at least 5 minutes. Fluff with fork. Serves 6.

NATALIE DUPREE'S SHRIMP
FROM: Bob Bennett

1 cup (2 sticks) butter
1 cup oil
2 tsps. finely chopped garlic
4 whole bay leaves, crushed
2 tsps. crushed rosemary
1/2 tsp. dried basil
1/2 tsp. oregano
1/2 tsp. salt
1/2 tsp. cayenne
1 TBL. paprika
3/4 tsp. freshly ground black pepper
1 tsp. fresh lemon juice
2 lbs. whole fresh shrimp in the shell

Melt butter, add oil, mix well. Add other ingredients except shrimp and cook over medium heat, stirring constantly, until sauce begins to boil. Reduce heat to low and simmer 7 to 8 minutes, stirring frequently. Then remove pan from heat and let stand uncovered at room temperature for at least 30 minutes to blend the flavors. Add shrimp to sauce, mix thoroughly. Put pan back on burner. Cook over medium heat until shrimp turns pink - about 5 or 6 minutes. Then put pan in preheated 450 degree oven and bake 10 minutes. Dish shrimp into 4 soup bowls, stirring the sauce as you ladle it into bowls. (Use everything in the pan, even the solid that settles to the bottom.) Eat with your hands and a soup spoon and plenty of paper napkins. (It is not nearly as flavorful cooked without the shells.) Makes 4-5 servings.

BARBEQUED SHRIMP
FROM: Sylvia Stanton

5 lbs. shrimp, heads on
1/2 lb. butter
1/2 box (small) whole peppercorns
1 tsp. salt

Butter bottom of a large 2" high 9" by 15" baking pan or glass dish. Wash shrimp, drain and place in bottom of dish. Place 2 sticks of butter on top of shrimp so that it will melt. Salt top of shrimp and sprinkle peppercorns over shrimp. Cook in a 325 degree oven for 20 minutes, stir, and cook for another 20 minutes. Serve with French bread so that your guests can dip into sauce or you can spread sauce on bread (It's like garlic bread). Serve shrimp hot and let everyone peel their own. A green salad is nice to serve with this.

CHINESE STYLE SHRIMP
FROM: the late Mills B. Lane

This is pretty and tastes good. Only salt we used was in boiling the shrimp.
1 TBL. olive oil
2 cloves garlic
1 8-oz. can pineapple chunks
1 to 1-1/2 TBLS. pickle juice
1 TBL. soy sauce
About 1/2 tsp. arrowroot dissolved in a little cold water
1/3 to 1/2 cup mixed sweet pickles, cut up
1 lb. shrimp, cooked, shelled and deveined
Medium tomato, cut in small chunks*
Cooked rice.

Heat oil with cracked garlic over high flame about 1 minute. Remove garlic. To avoid splatter, remove pan from heat while adding juice from pineapple can, juice from pickle jar and soy sauce. Return to heat and bring to boil. Add cut-up pickles and pineapple chunks. When it comes to boil again, thicken with arrowroot dissolved in cold water. Add shrimp and tomato chunks and cook about a minute or until warm through. Serve with rice. 4 servings.
*We peeled tomato after plunging into hot water.

SOUL SHRIMP
FROM: Diane McInnis

All measurements are estimates, arrived at for testing a generalized recipe. We felt it could be improved by tossing with butter and pepper like the Frogmore Stew recipe.

Ham hock
About 15 new potatoes, skins left on
1 medium onion, chopped
1 bag Crab Boil
1 TBL. vinegar
4 shakes of red pepper
3 lbs. of shrimp in shells
1/2 stick butter (optional)
1/2 tsp. pepper (optional)

Combine all except shrimp in salted water. Cover and boil until potatoes are tender. Add shrimp and boil a few minutes until shrimp are cooked. (When you see the meat pulling away from the shell, snatch them off the heat.) Keep covered 5 minutes. Drain. 6 to 8 servings.

SHRIMP FRIED RICE
FROM: Karen Weihs

3 cups or more boiled shrimp
3 cups diced celery
2 cups diced onion
3 cups large bell pepper
2 cups coarse grated carrot
1 block margarine
4 cups or more cooked rice
Soy sauce to taste

Saute vegetables and butter about 5 minutes on medium heat, stirring constantly. Put in shrimp, mix, then add rice. Mix well. Add salt, pepper and soy sauce to taste.
(Spoon out any excess moisture in vegetables before adding shrimp and rice.)

SHRIMP FRIED RICE
FROM: Mrs. Jackie Howard

As an extender, we used half the quantity of shrimp and cut them in small pieces, and the result was still delicious. Note shrimp and rice are prepared in advance.

3 lbs. raw shrimp
1-1/2 cups raw rice
Pat of butter
Salt & pepper
5 pieces bacon
1 onion, chopped
1 bell pepper, chopped
1 can mushroom pieces, drained and chopped
1 small can or jar pimientos, drained and chopped
2 TBLS. soy sauce
1 tsp. sugar
Salt & pepper
2 eggs, well beaten

Peel, devein and boil shrimp with preferred seasoning, using just enough water to cover shrimp. Drain and save "juice" (cooking water). Cook 1-1/2 cups rice in 2 cups of the shrimp juice to which butter, salt and pepper have been added. (This gives full shrimp flavor to the recipe). Rice should be cooked in advance for time to cool completely. Fry bacon in deep skillet until crisp. Crumble bacon and set aside. Saute onions, bell pepper and mushroom pieces in bacon fat in skillet. Add rice. Mix. Cook few minutes. Add shrimp, bacon pieces, pimientos, soy sauce, sugar, and salt and pepper to taste. Mix well. Add eggs and stir-cook until eggs are dry.

SHRIMP REMOULADE
FROM: Lynn Miller

3 lbs. medium shrimp, boiled, shelled and deveined
6 green onions
1 stalk celery
1 TBL. parsley
2 cloves garlic
5 TBLS. Creole Mustard (Zatarain's)
2 TBLS. paprika
2 tsps. horseradish
Salt (optional) and a little black pepper
1/3 cup vinegar
1/3 cup salad oil
1/3 cup olive oil
2/3 cup mayonnaise
Lemon wedges

Chop green onions, celery, parsley and garlic very fine or put
through a grinder. Add mustard, paprika, horseradish,
salt(optional), and pepper to onion, celery, parsley and garlic.
Pour in vinegar and mix well. Gradually add salad oil and then
olive oil until mixed thoroughly. Then stir in mayonnaise.
Marinate boiled, peeled shrimp in sauce at least 24 hours, the
longer the better. Serve on a bed of lettuce with fresh lemon as
a first course. If serving in one large bowl for a party, squeeze
on lemon juice before placing on lettuce leaves.

SEAFOOD CASSEROLE
FROM: the late Margaret Allan

1/2 lb. crabmeat
3/4 lb. small shrimp, raw (or cut up larger ones)
1 cup minced celery
2 green onions, minced fine with some tops
1 can water chestnuts, drained and diced
1 cup mayonnaise
Salt & Pepper
Bread crumbs
Butter
Combine first 6 ingredients. Put in casserole. Top with bread
crumbs and butter pats. Bake at 375 about 30 minutes or until
nice and bubbly. Serves 4.

AEGEAN SHRIMP
FROM: Denise Chetta

2 medium onions, sliced thinly
1/2 cup olive oil
1-1/2 lbs. fresh or canned tomatoes
4 cloves garlic, mashed
2 small bay leaves
2 tsps. oregano
1 tsp. basil
1/2 cup finely chopped fresh parsley
1 tsp. Chinese hot oil*
Salt & pepper
1-1/2 lbs. shrimp
1/2 lb. Feta cheese**
16 greek olives, halved
1 lemon

Saute onions in olive oil until tender. Add tomatoes, garlic, bay leaves, oregano, basil, parsley, hot oil and salt and pepper to taste. Cook 4-6 minutes. (If fresh tomatoes are used, cook for 12 minutes.) Peel, clean and cut shrimp in half, across the middle. Drain tomato/onion mixture and set aside. Return juice to saucepan, bring to a boil. Add shrimp, cook for 2 minutes, stirring constantly. Spread tomato evenly in a 10" by 8" baking dish. Arrange shrimp on top. Crumble Feta cheese and sprinkle. Arrange olive halves on top. Squeeze lemon. Place pan in 475 degree oven for 10-15 minutes. Serves 4 generously.
*Found in Publix oriental section.
**Original recipe called for 1 lb.

GRACE BUTLER'S SCAMPI
FROM: Centre Street Cookery

1 lb. large shrimp, peeled
1/2 stick butter
2 cloves garlic
1/2 tsp. salt
1/2 tsp. oregano
1/4 tsp. basil
3 TBLS. olive oil
1/2 cup coarsely chopped parsley
Parmesan and freshly ground pepper

Mince garlic; crush and blend with salt, oregano and basil. Heat butter, olive oil and garlic mixture in frying pan. When very hot, add shrimp and cook, stirring constantly, until shrimp are pink and firm. Add parsley and toss well. Sprinkle with Parmesan cheese and freshly ground pepper. Serve over rice.

ADELE'S SHRIMP AND CRAB CASSEROLE
FROM: Centre Street Cookery

2 6-oz. pkgs. wild and white rice mix
1 lb. fresh crabmeat
2 lbs. cooked shrimp, shelled and deveined
1 can mushroom soup, undiluted
1 can sliced mushrooms, drained
1/3 cup grated onion
1 cup chopped green pepper
1 cup chopped celery
1 4-oz. jar pimiento, drained and chopped
2 TBLS. lemon juice

Cook rice as directed. Lightly grease a 4-quart casserole. Preheat oven to 325 degrees. Combine all ingredients and mix gently, using crabmeat last. Bake one hour, uncovered. Reserve a few shrimp to garnish top. Serves 10-12.

CUBAN SHRIMP
FROM: *More Smorgasbord Secrets*

2 lbs. raw shrimp
1 cup olive oil (amount is correct)
1 large onion, chopped
1-2 green peppers, chopped
4-5 cloves garlic, minced
8 oz. tomato sauce
1/2 cup catsup
2/3 cup sherry
1 TBL. vinegar
5-6 bay leaves
1-1/2 tsps. salt
1 tsp. Accent
1/2 tsp. Tabasco
1 TBL. Worcestershire

Shell and devein shrimp; set aside. Put together what will be the basis for the sauce - the tomato sauce, catsup, sherry, vinegar and seasonings; add bay leaves and mix all together well. Saute shrimp in hot olive oil (just until pink), remove and reserve. Saute onion, green pepper and garlic in the olive oil, remove and reserve. Place all of the oil remaining in pan into the tomato mixture and stir with a whisk to incorporate the oil. Add shrimp and vegetables and mix all well. Place in refrigerator for shrimp to marinate in this mixture for several hours. Just before you are ready to serve, simmer the shrimp mixture for 20-25 minutes. Serve with plenty of toasted French bread (your guests will like this sauce!) and buttered rice, into which you have mixed chopped pimientoes and minced fresh parsley. Serves 4-6.

SHRIMP PIQUANTE
FROM: *More Smorgasbord Secrets*

2 lbs. jumbo shrimp
salt
pepper
mace
oregano
cayenne (optional)
paprika
lemon juice
garlic salt
butter or margarine
olive oil

Peel and devein shrimp. Place in flat baking dish and sprinkle on seasonings, light or heavy according to your taste. (Juice of 2 large lemons is suggested.) Cover the shrimp almost entirely with slices of butter or margarine about 1/4 inch thick. Dribble over all a small amount of olive oil (2-3 TBLS). Bake, uncovered, at 350 degrees for 30-40 minutes. Serve, with the juices, over brown rice. Serves 4.

SAUTEED ROCK SHRIMP
FROM: Peggy Higgins

Remove shells from 5 lbs. rock shrimp with scissors. Wash thoroughly under cold water to remove sand vein. Mix 2 TBLS. garlic salt, 1 TBL. parsley flakes, salt and pepper. Melt 4 TBLS. butter in iron skillet. Add some shrimp and sprinkle with proportionate part of seasoning. Toss shrimp in hot butter until they turn from grey to white (about 5 minutes). Repeat until all are cooked. Serve hot with drawn butter. Great with tossed salad and hot garlic bread.

SHRIMP CHOW MEIN
FROM: *Alone at the Range*

1 lb. shrimp, cooked*, peeled and sliced in half
1 green pepper cut in strips
1 red pepper, cut in strips
6 stalks celery, sliced
1/2 lb. mushroms, sliced
4 TBLS. butter
1 can bean sprouts, well drained
2 TBLS. soy sauce
2 TBLS. cornstarch
1 can chicken broth

Cook shrimp and put aside. Put butter in bottom of a large pan and melt. Steam the peppers, celery and mushrooms until soft. Add drained sprouts. In small pan heat broth and soy sauce. Thicken with cornstarch. Add to vegetables, add shrimp. Keep warm. Serve on Chinese rice noodles. Serves 4.
*To cook shrimp: bring 1 can of beer to a boil, drop in shrimp and boil for 2 minutes. Let shrimp sit in beer until cool.

SESAME SHRIMP
FROM: *Seafood - A Collection of Heart-Healthy Recipes*

1 TBL. margarine or olive oil
1 TBL. soy sauce
1/2 lb. shrimp, peeled and deveined
1 TBL. sesame seeds
1/4 cup green onions, diagonally cut
1/4 tsp. ground ginger or 1 tsp. fresh ginger, grated

Heat margarine or oil in skillet or wok. Add soy sauce, shrimp and sesame seeds. Cook over medium heat until shrimp is opaque, approx. 2-3 minutes. Stir in green onion and ginger. Heat thoroughly. Serve over wild rice. Makes 2 servings.

ROCK SHRIMP SAUTE
FROM: Gino Litrico

This recipe is recommended only if the Rock Shrimp are large because the preparation time is considerable. Experts say that, with kitchen scissors, you can cut the underside of the shell and slip the meat out intact. Using a sharp knife, we found it more efficient to do the reverse: cut the tough outside shell so you can spot and remove the sand vein more easily without tearing up the meat; starting at the head end, slip index finger between meat and shell and lift out two halves still attached at the top. Re-wash thoroughly and allow to drain dry. For 1-1/2 lbs. shelled Rock Shrimp, start with about 3 lbs. heads on.

2 TBLS. butter, melted
Splash of olive or vegetable oil
3 garlic cloves, mashed
1 chunk chopped fresh parsley
1/4 cup white wine or vermouth (optional)
1 TBL. flour
Minimal salt (optional)
1-1/2 lbs. shelled, deveined Rock Shrimp

Using a cast iron skillet, heat butter and oil. Keeping heat low, brown garlic slightly, add parsley and cook briefly. Add shrimp and stir around, covering well with butter, two or three minutes. Add wine. Cook a minute more. Thicken sauce with flour. Stir and coat shrimp well. Remove from heat, sprinkle with minimal salt (optional). Delicious with a good white wine.

SHRIMP AH-SO

FROM: *Southern Seafood Classics*

This beautiful cookbook was brought out by the Southern Fisheries Association. If all are as good as this recipe we tested, this book is a must in your kitchen.

1-1/2 lbs. raw, peeled, deveined shrimp
2 TBLS. salt
1 quart water
2 TBLS. soy sauce
1 tsp. cornstarch
1/2 tsp. garlic powder
1/2 tsp. ginger
1 can (1 lb.) unpeeled apricot halves, cut in half
2 fresh kiwifruit, peeled and cut into wedges (optional)
2 cups hot cooked rice
1/2 cup toasted slivered almonds
1/2 cup chopped parsley
Soy sauce

Thaw shrimp if frozen. Add salt to water and bring to a boil. Place shrimp in boiling water and reduce heat. Cover and simmer 3 to 4 minutes. Drain shrimp. Rinse under cold running water for 1 to 2 minutes. Combine soy sauce, cornstarch, garlic powder and ginger; shake together until thoroughly mixed. Drain apricots, reserving liquid. Combine apricot liquid and soy sauce mixture in a 10-inch skillet. Cook over medium heat, stirring constantly until thick and clear. Add shrimp, apricots and kiwifruit; cook over low heat for 1 to 2 minutes or until thoroughly heated. Combine hot rice, almonds and parsley. Serve shrimp mixture over almond rice. Serve with additional soy sauce if desired. Yield: 6 servings.

ELSIE McDOWELL'S BAKED SEAFOOD SALAD

FROM: *St. Mary's Seafood*

St. Mary's Seafood is a modest little cookbook that's chock full of good recipes. It is sold in Orange Hall at St. Mary's, Georgia.

1 can (7-1/2 oz.) flaked crab meat
1 can (4-1/2 oz.) shrimp or 1 lb. fresh cooked shrimp
1-1/2 cups chopped celery
1/4 cup chopped green pepper
1/4 cup chopped onion
1/4 cup chopped pimiento
1/2 tsp. Worcestershire sauce
1 tsp. salt
3/4 cup sour cream
1/4 cup mayonnaise
1 TBL. lemon juice
1 TBL. melted butter
Dash of pepper
1 cup bread crumbs

Combine crab meat, shrimp, celery, green pepper, onion and pimiento. Blend sour cream, lemon juice, mayonnaise, Worcestershire sauce, salt and pepper. Stir this into the seafood mixture. Spoon into 10 x 6 x 1-1/2 inch baking dish. Mix together bread crumbs and butter and sprinkle on top. Bake at 350 degrees 20 to 25 minutes. Serves 6 or 7.

CANLIS SHRIMP

This is adapted from the specialty of a Hawaiian restaurant. It's so simple, it's perfect.

2 lbs. large shrimp, shelled but tails left on
1 oz. olive oil
1 oz. butter
1 small garlic clove, crushed
1/4 tsp. salt
1/4 tsp. freshly ground black pepper
2 TBLS. lemon juice
2 TBLS. dry vermouth

Place oil in a large skillet. Heat. When it simmers, add shrimp and cook until almost done. Reduce heat, add butter, garlic, salt and pepper. When well blended, turn fire very hot. Add lemon juice and dry vermouth and cook about one minute, stirring constantly. Serves 6 to 8.

Crab

Whether you catch your own or buy them, crabs must be kept alive until they are cooked. Hence, you must have long-handled tongs to keep a safe distance from those pincers. Be sure the water comes to a full boil before you toss in the crabs. (If you put the crabs in first, as the water gets hotter, crabs start climbing out of the pot and skittering all over the kitchen.)

BOILED CRABS

Local blue crabs
Boiling water
1/2 cup salt
Zatarain's Crab Boil
2/3 cup vinegar
1 lemon

Fill a large enamel pot 2/3 full of water. Add salt and bring to full boil. Add vinegar, Crab Boil, lemon cut in half and squeezed to emit juice, and crabs. Boil about 20 minutes or until crabs turn bright red. Allow to cool in seasoned water. Serve with melted butter. To help you get at the goody, Florida's Department of Natural Resources has prepared instructions and diagrams on the following page:

To clean blue crab: 1) With crab upside down, grasp the legs on one side firmly with one hand, and with the other hand lift the flap (apron) and pull back and down to remove the top shell. 2) Turn the crab right side up, remove the gills and wash out the intestines and spongy material. 3) With a twisting motion pull the legs loose from the body. Remove any meat which adheres to the legs. Break off claws. 4) Slice off the top of the inner skeleton and remove all exposed meat on this slice. 5) At the back of the crab, on each side, lies a large lump of meat. With a very careful U-shaped motion of the knife, remove this back fin lump. 6) Remove the white flake meat from the other pockets with the point of the knife. 7) Crack the claw shell and remove the shell along with the moveable pincer. This will expose the claw meat and, if meat is left attached to the remaining pincer, will make a delicious (crab finger) hors d'oeuvre. Or the dark meat can be removed and used in soups, casseroles or salads.

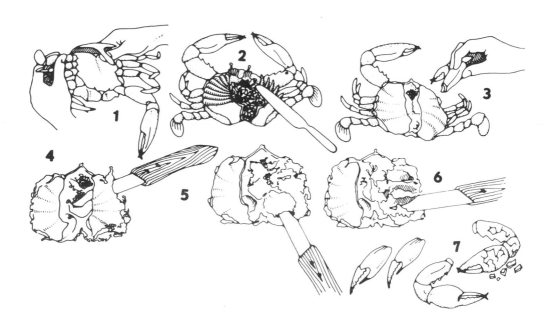

CRAB IMPERIAL
FROM: Karen Weihs

1 lb. white crabmeat
1 egg, beaten well
Dash of Tabasco or Worcestershire
Dash of black pepper
2 tsps. lemon juice
1/2 tsp. salt
1/2 cup mayonnaise

Lightly mix ingredients in large bowl. Put in casserole and top with crushed saltines or frozen tater tots. Dot with small pats of butter. Bake at 350 degrees for 25-30 minutes.

CONTENT PARTIN'S DEVILED CRAB
FROM: Centre Street Cookery

1 lb. crab meat
1/2 green pepper, chopped
1/4 cup catsup
2 TBLS. melted butter
1 egg, beaten
3/4 cup cracker meal
Salt and pepper (quite a bit of pepper)
1/2 small onion, grated
1/3 cup mayonnaise
Few drops Tabasco
1 TBL. Worcestershire sauce
1/4 cup milk

Mix all ingredients. Put into greased casserole. Pour melted butter on top. Cook at 375 degrees about half an hour.

LOUISE'S DEVILED CRAB
FROM: Centre Street Cookery

Louise Robinson Shafter was the cook for the late Judge James B. Stewart, Sr. This recipe was devised by the Judge's daughter, Frances Allen, by watching Louise at work.

2 cups crab meat
Juice of 1 lemon
3/4 cup saltine cracker crumbs
1 tsp. dry mustard
1 tsp. salt
3 hard-boiled eggs, chopped fine
2 TBLS. grated onion
1 tsp. Worcestershire
1 TBL. mayonnaise
1/2 tsp. white pepper

Use enough milk to moisten mixture. Place in crab shells or baking dish. Bake until brown in a 350 degree oven.

ANGELIC CRAB CAKES
FROM: Helen Litrico

1 egg, beaten
3 TBLS. mayonnaise
1/4 tsp. dry mustard
1 TBL. Worcestershire sauce
Dash hot pepper sauce
1 lb. claw crabmeat
1 TBL. fresh chopped parsley
Generous grating of nutmeg
1/2 tsp. salt
1/2 cup bread crumbs or cracker crumbs

Mix well beaten egg, mayonnaise, dry mustard, Worcestershire and hot pepper sauce. Add crabmeat, parsley, bread crumbs, nutmeg and salt. Chill in refrigerator before shaping. Dipping hands in water between times, shape into 8 small cakes and chill again about half an hour. Saute in small amount of hot olive or peanut oil about 3 minutes, turning to brown.

BORSHARD'S CRAB CAKES
FROM: Mary Borshard

1/2 lb. crabmeat
4 slices bread cut into small cubes
1/2 tsp. chopped parsley
1 scant tsp. lemon juice
2 TBLS. mayonnaise
2 eggs
1/2 tsp. grated onion

Fold ingredients in gently. Let stand in refrigerator 3 hours.
Place by large spoonfuls in hot butter. Brown on one side and
turn and brown on the other side. Cook on low heat for 5
minutes. Serve with lemon slices or tartar sauce. These can
also be frozen.

GILBERT MAGGIONI'S CRAB BURGERS
FROM: the late Mills B. Lane

*Crab burger recipe is the following Newburg stiffened with a very
little flour, then fried.*

Crab Newburg:
1/3 cup butter
3 TBLS. flour
1/2 tsp. salt
1/2 tsp. paprika
1 or 2 dashes tabasco
1/2 cup chopped parsley
3 large garlic buttons, chopped fine
1 TBL. Lea & Perrin's Worcestershire sauce
1-1/2 cups coffee cream
3 egg yolks, beaten
1 lb. crab meat
3 TBLS. sherry

Melt butter and blend in flour and seasonings. Add cream
gradually and cook until thick and smooth, stirring constantly.
Stir a little of this hot sauce into the egg yolk and add this to the
rest of the sauce, stirring constantly. Add crabmeat, then heat.
Remove from heat and stir in sherry slowly. Serve immediately
over toast.

CRAB POTATO CAKES
FROM: Eloise Blue

1 lb. fresh crabmeat
6 medium white potatoes
2 TBLS. butter or margarine
1/4 cup celery, chopped fine
1 medium onion, chopped fine
1/4 cup bell pepper, chopped
Salt & pepper
Accent (optional)
2 eggs
Flour or bread crumbs

Pick over crabmeat for shell. Peel, boil and dice potatoes.
Drain. Add hot potatoes and butter to crab, mash and mix well
with potato masher. Add celery, onion, bell pepper and
seasoning. Add 2 eggs last. Mix well. With greased fingers,
shape into cakes. Roll lightly in flour or bread crumbs. Deep fry
in Crisco over medium heat until golden brown. Serves 6.

CRAB POTS
FROM: Helen Litrico

1 lb. claw crabmeat
9 TBLS. milk (or Half & Half)
6 tsps. dry white wine
3 tsps. finely chopped green onion
6 to 12 drops Jalapeno Hot Sauce
Salt
1 cup unseasoned bread crumbs
6 TBLS. melted butter
Fine chopped parsley
Lime or lemon wedges

Pick over crab carefully to remove shell. Divide crab among 6
small ramekins. In each one, pour 1-1/2 TBLS. milk or Half &
Half, 1 tsp. wine, 1/2 tsp. green onion, 1 or preferably 2 drops of
hot sauce and a pinch of salt. Stir just enough to blend. Stir
crumbs into butter and scatter over crab. Bake uncovered in a
350 degree oven until lightly brown, about 25 minutes. Remove
from heat and sprinkle with chopped parsley. Serve with lemon
or lime wedges. Serves 6.

EDNA'S CRABMEAT CASSEROLE
FROM: Mrs. Billie Hart

1 lb. crabmeat, picked over for shell pieces
8 TBLS. butter
4 TBLS. flour
2 cups milk
4 tsps. lemon juice
2 tsps. dry mustard
2 tsps. salt
4 hard boiled eggs, chopped
1 cup mayonnaise
Onion to taste
1 tsp. Worcestershire sauce
1/2 tsp. seasoning salt
Dash white pepper (optional)
Dash Tabasco
1 cup drained sliced mushrooms (optional)

Make a cream sauce with butter, flour and milk. Add remaining ingredients. Place in long flat baking dish. Top with bread crumbs (or finely crumbled cheese crackers). Sprinkle with Parmesan cheese and dot with butter and dash of paprika. Bake at 350 degrees until bubbly and lightly brown.

CRAB SALAD A LA MOSCA
FROM: Helen & Gino Litrico

Leaf Lettuce (enough to fill a large salad bowl)
1 stalk celery, cut up
12 ripe black or unstuffed green olives, sliced
8 TBLS. rice vinegar seasoned for salad
3 TBLS. top quality olive oil
1 lb. crab meat, picked over

Break leaf lettuce into bite-sized pieces. Add celery and olives and mix. In separate little bowl mix rice vinegar and oil. Pour over lettuce mixture and toss. Then add crab meat and toss gently and serve. 12 little appetizers or 4 main course dishes.

VERSATILE CRAB
FROM: Helen Litrico

This is adapted from Hon Versaggi's recipe for Crab Casserole. To use as a dip, she omits egg and bread crumbs. We omit the topping of bread crumbs and just dot top with butter to bake as stuffing for 8 dozen of Mrs. Skipper's little pastry shells. We also rolled the raw mix up in Crescent Dinner Roll dough and baked for a Sunday brunch entree.

2 large onions, chopped fine
1 can of cream of mushroom soup
1 lb. crabmeat
1/4 cup parsley, chopped fine
Little over 1/2 cup bread crumbs
1 whole egg
Pepper, Tabasco or other hot sauce to taste
1/4 cup grated Parmesan & Romano cheese

Wilt onions in oil or butter. Add crabmeat, soup, parsley, bread crumbs, seasoning, egg and cheese. Put in buttered casserole, top with Italian bread crumbs and dot with butter. Bake at 375 degrees for about 30 minutes. Serves 6.

CRABMEAT NORFOLK
FROM: Lynn Miller

1 lb. jumbo lump crabmeat
1/2 stick butter
1 bunch green onions, chopped
1/3 cup chopped parsley
Juice of 1/2 lemon
Granulated garlic to taste
Salt & Pepper to taste

Melt butter in saute pan. Add onions and cook 5 minutes. Add remaining ingredients and cook until hot. Transfer to heated individual ramekins.

CRAB CRISTO
FROM: Helen Litrico

12 slices bread, crusts trimmed off
4 eggs, beaten
1/2 cup milk
3/4 to 1 stick butter
3 green onions, thinly sliced including some green part
1 stalk celery, chopped fine
1/2 lb. crabmeat
1/2 cup mayonnaise
1 TBL. chopped, fresh parsley
Salt
White pepper
1 TBL. Worcestershire sauce
Dash Tabasco
6 slices Swiss cheese

Make French toast. Add milk to beaten eggs, dip bread into egg mixture and then brown in melted butter in skillet. It will take at least half a stick of butter. Drain bread on paper towels. Put a quarter stick of butter in skillet and saute green onions and celery until limp. Add crab and heat. Mix crab-onion-celery with mayonnaise, parsley and seasonings. Put on French toast, add slice of Swiss cheese, top with another slice of French toast. Heat in electric grill until cheese is melted. Serves 6 as entree or cut into quarters for hors d'oeuvres.

CRAB PIE

FROM: Phyllis Stoddard

1-1/2 cups herb seasoned Pepperidge Farm dressing
3/4 cup butter
3 TBLS. minced green onions
1/4 cup flour
1-1/2 cups milk
1 lb. crabmeat
2 TBLS. minced pimiento
1/4 tsp. dry mustard
Salt & pepper
1/2 cup sour cream
Minced fresh parsley

Roll stuffing mix to make fine crumbs and mix with 1/2 cup melted butter. Press firmly against bottom and sides of 9" pie pan. Saute onion tops in 1/4 cup butter; add flour and blend, stirring constantly. Gradually add milk and cook, stirring until the sauce is smooth and thick. Add crabmeat, pimiento, mustard, salt and pepper. Stir in sour cream. Turn into pie pan and bake about 20 to 25 minutes in a 375 degree oven.

Fish & Other Seafood

GRAVLAX
FROM: Sperry Lee

Large bunch of fresh dillweed
2 TBLS. of salt and 3/4 TBL. of sugar mixed in a small bowl
4-5 TBLS. brandy
2 large salmon fillets with skin intact

Remove any bones that remain in the fillets. Use a glass dish (2 or 3 quart pyrex) large enough for fish to fit in. Place a layer of fresh dill in bottom of dish. Place one fillet skin side down on top of dill. Place other fillet skin side down on a work surface next to dish. Rub top sides of each fillet with the salt and sugar mixture. Sprinkle with brandy. Place a layer of dill over fillet in dish and place second fillet over it - flesh to flesh. Cover with more dill. Place plastic wrap over dish. Place a board or other flat object over the fillets, then place a brick or other weight (such as a 5 lb. bag of sugar) on the board or other cover so as to compress the fillets. Place dish in refrigerator. After three days, sample. Add salt mixture and brandy as needed. Flip fillets so that the bottom one is on top and top one on bottom. Replace in refrigerator covered and weighted for three more days. Then, slice thin and serve.

MARINADE FOR GRILLED FISH
FROM: Gino Litrico

3 TBLS. olive oil
2 TBLS. lemon juice
2 TBLS. dry vermouth
1/2 tsp. dry mustard
1/2 tsp. jalapeno sauce

Dust 3 to 4 medium fish with black pepper, white pepper, dill and oregano. Let sit about 20 minutes. Prepare marinade and marinate fish 20 minutes or more. Cook on grill in turner sprayed with Pam.

SAUTEED TROUT
FROM: Gino Litrico

Sprinkle skinned trout fillets with black pepper, white pepper and thyme and let rest. Make marinade of 1/2 cup olive oil, 1/4 cup lemon juice, one-plus TBLS. of White Wine Worcestershire and 1 tsp. soy sauce. Blend well. Place trout fillets in marinade 10 or 20 minutes. Dredge fillets slightly in flour. Saute in butter over medium heat until brown. Remove. Add marinade to butter in skillet. Cook briefly and pour as sauce over fish fillets.

SAUTEED FLOUNDER FILLETS
FROM: Gino Litrico

In preparing this batter, regular kitchen spoons are used rather than measuring spoons.

Boneless, skinless flounder fillets for 4
Black Pepper
White Pepper
Thyme
1 egg, beaten
1/4 cup water
2 heaping TBLS. flour
1 TBL. soy sauce
1 tsp. Worcestershire sauce
2 TBLS. oil
1 tsp. dried parsley flakes
1 TBL. cornstarch
2 TBLS. plain bread crumbs
Oil and butter

Season fillets with peppers and thyme and let sit. In small bowl, mix batter of next 9 ingredients and stir with whisk. Pour into wide, shallow bowl. Dredge fillets in batter mix and let sit in same bowl to marinate. Heat oil and butter. When about to brown, shake excess batter from fillets and saute in oil-butter until golden brown. Serves 4.

GRILLED CURRIED SEAFOOD
FROM: Gino Litrico

This can be shrimp, scallops, squid or fish but preferably a combination of at least two kinds of seafood.

Clean and prepare seafood. If using squid or fish, cut into bite sizes. Drain well. Put in bowl and dust with generous sprinklings of turmeric and curry powder, skimpy dashes of granulated garlic, pepper, salt, paprika and chili powder. Let sit 20 or 30 minutes. Pour olive oil in skillet and add little bit of butter. Melt butter. Let skillet cool and put seasoned seafood in with oil and butter and mix. Let sit 30 minutes or an hour. Put small screen mesh on grill and spray with Pam. Grill, turning with tongs. (This can also be cooked under a broiler or sauteed.)

CRABMEAT STUFFING FOR BAKED FISH
FROM: the late Margaret Allan

1/4 cup minced white bacon (salt pork)
1/3 cup minced green onion
1 level TBL. very finely minced green pepper
1/2 cup fine unseasoned bread crumbs (can use plain
Pepperidge Farm mix)
1 lemon, squeezed & grated
1 tsp. dry mustard
1 egg, stirred
1 lb. claw crabmeat
Salt & pepper

Saute white bacon until rendered but not brown. Add onion and green pepper. Cook very slowly till soft. Remove from heat and add all other ingredients except crab. Mix well with light tosses. Add crabmeat and blend well. Stuff into cavity of oven-ready big fish and put extra along belly side of fish.

GRILLED OR BROILED BLUEFISH
FROM: Gino Litrico

Bluefish is the most under-appreciated fish around. True, it demands some care in that it should be chilled immediately after it is caught, but it is extremely healthful (an oily fish), and it tastes delicious cooked this way.

Score fish. Dust with white pepper, black pepper, thyme, ginger, oregano and scant garlic powder. Let sit 10 or 15 minutes. Make marinade of 1/4 cup olive oil, 1/4 cup lemon juice, few dashes soy sauce, few dashes white wine Worcestershire and a scant dash of regular Worcestershire. Put fish in marinade. Turn, baste and let marinate 15 or 20 minutes. Then grill or broil. This is also a good way to do Spanish mackerel, salmon steaks and chicken breasts.

DIETER'S BAKED FISH
FROM: Gino Litrico

Sprinkle oven-ready fish with black pepper and a little oregano. Spray shallow baking pan with Pam. (Optional: put a layer of thinly sliced potatoes, add 1/4 inch water, cover and pre-cook 20 minutes.) Put fillets in pan, then layer of thinly sliced onions, then layer of sliced tomatoes. Just bless the top with a little oregano and squeeze half a lemon over all. Add a little water (if not put in with potatoes). Cover. Bake in 450 degree oven until onions are wilting. Add half cup dry white wine and cover. Bake 'til alcohol burns off and onions are done. If too much liquid remains, remove cover and bake at 500 for a few minutes.

SIMPLE BAKED FISH FILLET
FROM: Alone at the Range

1 flounder fillet
1/4 cup bread crumbs
1/4 cup Parmesan cheese
1 TBLS. mayonnaise

Combine bread crumbs and cheese on paper towel. Spread mayonnaise on both sides of fish. Coat fish with bread crumb mixture. Place on double thickness of waxed paper, cover with waxed paper. Micro 4 minutes.

SAVANNAH KINGFISH
FROM: Mary Holt Boswell

Cut fish into small pieces, 2" by 2" or thereabouts. Place in shallow dish and marinate in dry vermouth 2-3 hours. Turn once. To cook: Place in shallow baking dish and pour over it 1/2 stick butter, melted, with the juice of a lemon. Bake at 450 degrees until done.
Sauce: Meanwhile, make cream sauce of 2 TBLS. butter and 2 TBLS. flour, 1 cup liquid consisting of milk, dry vermouth from marinade, and juice from small can of mushrooms. Add mushrooms when done. To Serve: Put in serving dish and pour mushroom sauce over. Garnish with a sprig of parsley. Good served with rice.

BAKED RED BASS
FROM: Helen Litrico

May use red bass or any other non-oily fish.

Drain fish, pat dry with paper towels. Score both sides with 2 or 3 cuts. Salt and pepper well, inside and out. Line a large, shallow, buttered baking dish with thick slices of baking potato. Preheat oven to 450 degrees while you stuff fish cavity with layers of onion rings, sliced tomato, bell pepper strips, pats of butter and sprigs of parsley. Salt and pepper vegetable stuffing. Heat baking dish while you sew up or skewer fish. Place fish in baking dish, putting any extra vegetables at the head. Put lemon slices on top. Cover with foil. Cook at 450 degrees about 15 minutes. Then reduce heat to 350 degrees. Pour a cautious amount of white wine over and baste with juices. Cook about 1 hour or until done, basting occasionally. (Fish is done when meat is opaque and milk-colored.)

SHARK ORIENTAL

Shark is great eating, believe it! Florida's home economist, Sue Turner has been promoting it for years. We tried it, liked it for its delicate flavor, and there are no bones except the center backbone. Shark should be small (preferably under 40 lbs.) and absolutely fresh when frozen or cooked. Our favorite recipe comes from a Susan Cleveland of Camden, Maine.

2 lbs. shark, swordfish or halibut
1/4 cup orange juice
1/4 cup soy sauce
2 TBLS. catsup
2 TBLS. melted butter
2 TBLS. chopped parsley
1 TBL. lemon juice
1 clove garlic
1/2 tsp. oregano
1/2 tsp. pepper

Place fish steaks in single layer in shallow pan. Make sauce of other ingredients. Pour over fish and let stand 30 minutes, turning once after 15 minutes. Remove fish steaks and place on greased broiler pan. Depending on thickness, broil 5 minutes per side but keep an eye on it. Baste frequently with reserve sauce. Can be done outdoors on well-greased charcoal grill. Serves 6.

HERB BAKED GROUPER
FROM: the late Agnes Olmstead

We varied this recipe by putting the onions on top of the fish and putting thin-sliced potatoes under the fish to prevent sticking.

1 to 1-1/4 lbs. thin grouper fillets
1 cup thinly sliced onions
2/3 cup mayonnaise
1/3 cup grated Parmesan cheese
1 TBL. tarragon vinegar
1 TBL. finely cut fresh parsley
1 tsp. finely cut fresh tarragon or basil (or 1/2 tsp. dried tarragon leaves)
Paprika

Wash grouper; cut into 4 serving portions; pat dry. Lightly butter a 13 x 9 inch baking pan. Separate onions into rings and arrange them to cover bottom of pan. Place grouper on top. Stir together remaining ingredients except paprika. Evenly spread this over grouper. Sprinkle with paprika. Bake in moderate oven, 350 degrees, 20 to 25 minutes or until fish flakes evenly with a fork. If desired, place under broiler to lightly brown. Makes 4 servings.

SAUTEED FISH FILLETS
FROM: Charles Litrico

Marinade:
>1 egg
>1 tsp. soy sauce
>1 oz. vermouth
>1 oz. water

Pat fish dry and sprinkle with black and white pepper to taste. Dust fillets in flour. Place fish in marinade and let soak for about 15 minutes, turning occasionally. Sprinkle lightly with bread crumbs just prior to cooking. Preheat skillet with olive oil and butter. Cook until light golden brown.

FISH QUICHE
FROM: Anne and Katherine Coonrod

2 unbaked pie shells
2 cups cooked flaked fish (leftovers are fine)
1 can mushroom soup
3 eggs
1 2-oz. can chopped mushroom pieces
1/2 onion, chopped
1 tsp. lemon pepper
1 tsp. lemon juice
1 TBL. Worcestershire sauce
Salt to taste
1 cup grated Swiss cheese

Layer half of cheese in bottom of pie shells. Mix all other ingredients and fill pie crusts. Top with other half of cheese and sprinkle with paprika. Bake at 350 degrees for 40 to 50 minutes. A great luncheon treat. May be prepared ahead and warmed at time of serving. Great use for leftover fish or inexpensive cuts such as rib rolls, fish fingers or back bones.

BAKED COBIA ROE
FROM: Anne Coonrod / the late Mills B. Lane

Divide roe into two pieces. Put butter, lemon juice, salt and pepper on each with a bacon slice on top. Bake 25 minutes. Turn on broiler briefly to crisp bacon.

CAPER SAUCE
FROM: Andre Perez

In cast iron skillet, make a roux of 2 to 3 TBLS. olive oil and 3 to 4 TBLS. flour. Thin with dry white wine. Sprinkle in Everglades Seasoning and close to half a small jar of capers. Serve over cooked fish or chicken.

INLAND PAELLA

FROM: More Smorgasboard Secrets

Find this and many other good recipes in this cookbook published by the women of St. Peter's Episcopal Church.

4 TBLS. olive oil
4 whole chicken breasts, split
8 chicken thighs
3-4 medium onions, chopped
5-6 garlic cloves, chopped
2 cups uncooked rice
1-1/2 lbs. smoked link sausage
5 cups chicken broth
Pinch of saffron (dissolve in broth)
1 7-oz. can clams, undrained
1-1/2 lbs. shrimp, cooked and cleaned
1 8-oz. can Leseur peas, drained
1 4-oz. jar pimientos, drained and chopped
Salt and white pepper to taste

Prick sausage thoroughly and poach gently in water to cover on top of stove for about 10 minutes. Drain, slice in one-inch pieces and set aside. Heat oil in large skillet and quickly brown batches of chicken. Place chicken in large, lightly oiled oven-to-table casserole and set aside. Add more oil to the saute pan if necessary and saute onions and garlic; add rice and saute until it is golden, then add all to the casserole.Salt and pepper at this point, then add the sliced sausages and stir to distribute all. Pour over the mixture four cups of broth in which the saffron was dissolved; reserve one cup. Cover casserole and bake at 325 degrees for about one hour or until chicken is tender. (Check liquid after 30 minutes and add more broth if needed.) Just before the cooking period is over, add clams and their juice and the cooked shrimp; stir gently to distribute. At serving time, correct seasonings and sprinkle peas and pimiento bits over top of casserole. (Other seafoods, particularly chunks of well seasoned poached fish and lump crabmeat, add interesting taste and texture variations to this recipe.) Serves 8 amply.

CUCUMBER-DILL SAUCE FOR FISH
FROM: National Fisherman (Clare Vanderbeek)

1 large cucumber, peeled, seeded and finely chopped
1 cup sour cream
1/3 cup plain, low-fat yogurt
2 TBLS. mayonnaise
1-1/2 tsp. dried dill weed (or 2-3 TBLS. finely chopped fresh dill)
1/8 tsp. salt
Dash freshly ground pepper
Dash hot pepper sauce

Combine all ingredients. Chill thoroughly. Serve hot or cold
with broiled, steamed or baked fish. Makes about 2 cups.

AVOCADO SALSA FOR FISH
FROM: National Fisherman (Clare Vanderbeek)

1 tomato, peeled, seeded and finely chopped
1/4 cup canned, chopped mild green chiles
2 TBLS. chopped green onion
1 to 2 tsps. finely chopped cilantro or parsley
2 tsps. oil
1-1/2 tsps. lime or lemon juice
1 avocado, diced
Salt and freshly ground pepper

Combine tomato, chiles, green onion, parsley, oil and lime juice.
Season to taste with salt and pepper. Gently stir in avocado
within 2 hours of serving. Serve sauce at room temperature with
hot or cold baked or broiled fish. Makes 1-1/2 cups.

FIRST COURSE OYSTERS
FROM: Lynn Miller

Saute 2 cloves minced garlic and 1 TBL. chopped parsley in 1/3 stick butter. Add 1 pint oysters, 1/4 tsp. oregano, large pinch of crushed rosemary leaves and cook until oysters curl. Remove to individual ramekins and top with seasoned bread crumbs and Romano cheese. Heat in a 400 degree oven for 10 minutes and then place under broiler until browned. Serve with crisp French bread to dip in sauce. Serves 4.

OYSTER GRAVY
FROM: Mrs. Emmett Freeman

Mrs. Freeman says this is not suitable with processed oysters because her secret is that the oyster meat is never washed by fresh water.

Fresh oysters in shells
White bacon (unsmoked salt pork) cut very thin
Flour
Salt and pepper
Corn meal (optional)
Rice or grits

Scrub outside of oyster shells thoroughly. Then shuck carefully to keep from spilling juices. Wash oysters back and forth in their own juices. (That is - put oysters in strainer and drain juices into bowl; lift out oysters, put into juice, and wipe sand and shell out of strainer. Repeat several times.) Warm juice on stove and skim off scum on top. Set aside. Fry white bacon until golden. Drain off excess fat, leaving bacon in pan. Add a little flour and brown. Add oyster juice, salt and pepper. Let come to a good simmer and add oysters. When bag part of oyster is firm, take them off, as gravy should be thick enough. Serve on grits or rice.
VARIATION: Thicken oyster juice with a little sifted corn meal of the old-fashioned water ground type.

SCALLOPED OYSTERS
FROM: Mrs. Cynthia Parks

1 quart oysters
1 cup croutons or Pepperidge Farm's dressing crumbs
2 cups cracker crumbs (not Saltines)
1 cup butter (2 sticks)
Salt & Pepper
8 TBLS. oyster liquid
4 TBLS. cream
Nutmeg

Melt butter in skillet. Toss crumbs until saturated. Press 1/3 crumbs in shallow buttered dish. Cover with half the oysters. Sprinkle with salt, pepper and a dash of nutmeg. Add 4 TBLS. liquid and 2 TBLS. cream. Repeat performance. Cover top with crumbs. Bake at 450 degrees for 30 minutes.

OYSTER PIE
FROM: Mrs. Bea Lyons

2 oz. white bacon (unsmoked salt pork)
1 quart fresh oysters
Salt and pepper
Dough for 2 pie crusts
Crushed saltine crackers
Butter

Cut white bacon in cubes and fry. Add oysters and stir and cook just a minute. Remove from heat. Season with salt and pepper. Use frozen pie crust or make from scratch. Put one crust in a 350 degree oven about 5 minutes. Take out and put into crust one layer of crushed saltines, layer of oysters, and repeat layers to fill. Put other pie crust on top, prick with fork and dot with butter. Bake in 350 degree oven until brown.

OYSTER PILAU
FROM: Mrs. Bea Lyons

4 oz. white bacon (unsmoked salt pork)
1 medium onion, chopped
1/2 bell pepper, chopped (optional)
1 quart fresh oysters
Salt and pepper
2 cups water
2 cups raw rice, washed

Drain oysters. Cut white bacon in cubes and fry. Add chopped onion. Add oysters and stir a little so barely cooks. Add 2 cups of water, salt and pepper to taste. Add 2 cups raw rice. Turn to medium heat and let boil until water almost boils out. Turn very low until rice gets done. Serves 4.

OYSTER FRITTERS
FROM: Mrs. Bea Lyons

1 quart fresh oysters
Pancake mix
1 egg, beaten
Salt & pepper

Drain oysters and put in mixing bowl. Add beaten egg and enough pancake mix to hold together. Add salt and pepper. Drop spoonful at a time into deep hot fat. Cooks in just a few minutes.

CLAM SAUCE FOR SPAGHETTI
FROM: Enzo Brisciano

2 TBLS. real butter
1 small can minced clams
2 cloves garlic, minced
Chunk of fresh parsley, chopped fine
Salt, pepper, Accent

Saute all ingredients in butter. Add 1 to 2 tsps. water if needed. When comes to boil, turn low and simmer until thick. Drain cooked spaghetti. Mix most of sauce with spaghetti. Serve extra sauce on side. 2-3 servings.

Chicked

CHICKEN CACCIATORE
FROM: Mrs. Joanna Litrico

1 chicken, cut in quarters
Salt
Oil
1 large onion, chopped
2 tender stalks celery, cut in bite-size pieces
1 cup combined green olives and capers*
Salt & pepper
About 2 oz. white vinegar

Clean chicken and salt. Let drain in colander 5-10 minutes. Cut in pieces. Saute in oil on both sides. Remove chicken. Saute chopped onion, then add celery, then olives and capers. Cook about 5 minutes, stirring. Put chicken back in. Add salt, pepper and vinegar. Cook, covered, over slow flame, watching and stirring occasionally about 45-50 minutes. May need to add a little water.
*Use unstuffed green olives or remove centers from stuffed ones. Ratio is about three-fourths olives, one-fourth capers.

ZIA'S GRILLED CHICKEN
FROM: Agata Rizzo

Oil
A little vinegar
Onion, sliced in rings
2 cloves garlic, mashed
Rosemary (generous amount)
Sage (couple pinches)
Boned chicken breasts

Make marinade of first six ingredients. Marinate chicken breasts for 2 hours. Grill over low coals, basting with marinade.

CHICKEN ROSEMARY
ADAPTED FROM: Craig Claiborne

1 tsp. dried or 1 TBL. fresh rosemary
2 tsps. white wine vinegar
3 TBLS. olive oil
1/4 stick butter
3 medium onions, finely minced
1 small clove garlic, minced
1 2-1/2 to 3 lb. frying chicken, cut into serving pieces
Salt and freshly ground pepper to taste
1/2 cup dry vermouth
1/2 cup water
2 tsps. parsley, finely minced
1/2 cup chopped cooked ham

Skin as much of chicken as possible. (I pass on skinning wings.) Pat dry. Soak rosemary in the vinegar. Melt butter and olive oil in a skillet. Heat slowly until foamy. Add onions and garlic and saute until golden. Add chicken pieces (usually done in two batches) to skillet and saute over medium heat until an opaque white with a little browning. (Skinned chicken doesn't brown as much as that with skin.) Add the vinegar and rosemary, salt and pepper. Combine the vermouth and water and add to chicken. Sprinkle with minced parsley. Cover and cook until done, about 30 minutes. Five minutes before the chicken is ready, add ham. Serves 4.

PEPPERCORN CHICKEN BREASTS
FROM: Phyllis Maines

1 TBL. whole black peppercorns
3/4 tsp. thyme
1 small bay leaf, broken
4 chicken breast halves, skinned, boned and flattened
1/4 tsp. salt
3 TBLS. minced shallots or white part of green onions
2 cloves garlic, peeled and halved lengthwise
1 TBL. butter or margarine
1 TBL. chopped fresh parsley
1/3 cup dry white wine

In blender or food processor, process peppercorns, thyme and bay leaf until peppercorns are coarsely cracked and bay leaf is no longer discernible. Sprinkle both sides of chicken with salt, pepper mixture, shallots and garlic, pressing lightly so seasonings cling. Cover with waxed paper and let stand at room temperature 2 hours. Discard garlic. Saute chicken in butter, turning and lowering heat to get inside done. Remove to serving plate. Sprinkle with chopped parsley. Add wine to pan drippings and cook at high heat, stirring often, 2 minutes or until liquid reduced to 3 TBLS. Spoon over chicken. Garnish with parsley sprigs.

CHICKEN REUBEN
Adapted from a TV recipe

Half of a 2-lb. pkg. of fresh sauerkraut
Scant 1/4 tsp. caraway seeds
4 boneless breasts of chicken
White pepper, black pepper, thyme and (optional) salt
Sliced Swiss cheese to cover
1/2 cup Thousand Island Dressing

Drain sauerkraut. Skin and season chicken with white pepper, black pepper, thyme and (optional) salt. Put sauerkraut in bottom of casserole and sprinkle caraway seeds over. Then layer in chicken breasts and add Swiss cheese to cover. Bake covered in a 350 degree 45 minutes. Remove from oven, add Dressing, cover again and let sit until Dressing is warm.

PEPPERY CHICKEN BREASTS
FROM: Gino Litrico

Dust chicken breast halves, boned and skinned, with:

Black pepper
Adolph's Natural Tenderizer
Ground ginger
Crushed rosemary
Crushed green peppercorns, pressed into the meat

Poke breasts with fork. Let sit 15 or 20 minutes.
Combine marinade of:

1/4 cup olive or vegetable oil
1/8 cup lemon juice
2 dashes Worcestershire sauce
2 dashes soy sauce
3-4 dashes White Wine Worcestershire
4-5 dashes Trappey's Chef-Magic Jalapeno Sauce*

Marinate chicken about 25 minutes, turning and poking with fork
occasionally. Then grill, basting with marinade from time to
time.
*Can substitute the green Louisiana hot sauce.

OVEN BARBEQUED CHICKEN
FROM: Rosalie Versaggi

This is adapted from a dish served at Prudhomme's Cajun Cafe in Louisiana.

2 tsps. marjoram
1 tsp. paprika
1/2 tsp. salt
1/2 tsp. granulated garlic
1/4 tsp. white pepper
1/4 tsp. red pepper
1/4 tsp. black pepper
1 cut-up frying chicken or preferred parts for 4 servings
2/3 cup onion, finely chopped
1/3 cup green onion, finely chopped
1/2 cup green pepper, finely chopped
2 cups chicken stock or water
1/2 small can tomato paste
1 TBL. Worcestershire sauce
1 tsp. Dijon mustard
1/2 tsp. brown sugar
1/2 tsp. lemon juice
1/8 tsp. salt

Clean chicken and remove as much skin and fat as possible. Combine first 7 ingredients in small bowl and mix well. Sprinkle **half** the seasoning over both sides of chicken and place in a baking dish that has been sprayed with Pam. Set aside. Spray the inside of a small skillet with Pam and place over medium heat. Add onion and green pepper; cook and stir 1 minute. Add remaining seasoning mix and all remaining ingredients. Cook 15 minutes, stirring often. Remove from heat; baste chicken with sauce and bake in a 350 degree oven for 50 minutes or until tender, basting chicken often. Serves 4.

CHICKEN KIEV WITH SHRIMP
FROM: Mrs. Mary Hill

Mary says a Valdosta cook won a national prize with this recipe. We'd love to credit her if we knew her name.

6 large chicken breasts
1/2 cup chopped green onion
2 TBLS. chopped parsley (Editor's addition)
1 cup shrimp, cooked and chopped
1 stick real butter, softened
Salt and pepper
1 egg
Flour
Plain bread crumbs

Boil shrimp in usual seasonings; allow to cool in water. Shell, devein, chop and sprinkle with lemon juice. Combine softened butter, chopped shrimp, parsley and green onion. Wrap in wax paper and form into six inch roll. Chill in freezer until very firm. Bone chicken breasts and flatten to 1/4" thickness. Cut butter - shrimp roll into 6 equal parts. Place a portion on each chicken breast. Tuck sides in and roll up breast tightly, completely enclosing butter mixture. Secure with string or skewers. Dredge rolls in flour. Chill at least 30 minutes. Dip in beaten egg; drain and coat with bread crumbs. Let dry 5 minutes. Repeat egg and crumb coating. Chill another 30 minutes. Fry chicken rolls in 2 inches of hot oil about 12 minutes or until brown, turning occasionally. Drain and let cool a bit before serving.

CHICKEN MARBELLA
FROM: Barbara Benisch

This is adapted from a recipe created by The Silver Palate, a gourmet take-out deli in New York. Great for a party, it is presented in quantities to serve 10 or 12 but is easily divided to make smaller amounts. The overnight marination is essential, and the flavor improves if refrigerated several days. Original recipe did not call for skinning chicken.

4 chickens, 2-1/2 lbs. each, quartered (we prefer getting 8 leg quarters and 8 breasts with ribs - no wings)
1 head of garlic, peeled and finely pureed
1/4 cup dried oregano
Salt and freshly ground black pepper to taste
1/2 cup red wine vinegar
1/2 cup olive oil
1 cup pitted prunes
1/2 cup pitted Spanish green olives
1/4 cup capers with a bit of juice
6 bay leaves
1 cup brown sugar
1 cup white wine
1/4 cup Italian parsley or cilantro, finely chopped

Skin chicken pieces (optional) and pat dry. Arrange pieces in a single layer in two large shallow baking pans. Combine garlic, oregano, pepper, salt, vinegar, olive oil, prunes, olives, capers and juice and bay leaves. Spread evenly over chicken, cover and let marinate, refrigerated, overnight.
Preheat oven to 350 degrees. Sprinkle chicken pieces with brown sugar and pour white wine around them. Bake 50 minutes to an hour, basting frequently with pan juices. Serve from the baking pan with a ladle to get pan juices to moisten chicken and pour over rice or, with a slotted spoon, transfer chicken, prunes, olives and capers to a serving platter, moisten with a few spoonfuls of pan juices and pass remaining pan juices in a sauceboat. Sprinkle parsley or cilantro over chicken. Serves 10 or 12 generously.

SPANISH CHICKEN
FROM: Helen Litrico

*This basic recipe appeared in Sunset magazine many years
ago. Original did not call for skinning chicken.*

3 or 4 TBLS. olive oil or salad oil
6 whole chicken legs and thighs (or breasts with ribs - no wings)
1/2 cup chopped onion
2 cloves garlic, minced or mashed
2 TBLS. all-purpose flour
1 can (1 lb.) tomatoes
1/2 tsp. grated orange peel
1 tsp. each ground cinnamon and sugar
1/4 cup red wine (optional)
Salt and Pepper
1/2 cup each golden raisins and pitted ripe olives

Skin chicken (optional). Heat oil in a large frying pan over
medium heat; add the chicken pieces and brown well on all
sides. Transfer chicken to a shallow 3-quart casserole. Add
onion and garlic to the pan and saute until onion is limp. Stir in
flour and cook until bubbly; add tomatoes (breaking them up
with a spoon), orange peel, cinnamon, sugar, wine (optional),
and salt and pepper to taste. Cook, stirring until thickened.
Pour sauce over chicken, cover, and bake in a 350 degree oven
for 50 minutes. Uncover, skim fat if necessary, and sprinkle in
olives and raisins; bake, covered, 10 minutes longer. Serves 6.

POLLO CON RIZZO E UVA SECA
(Chicken with Rice and Raisins)
FROM: Joanna Litrico

1/2 cup olive oil or Mazola
1 3 to 3-1/2 lb. fryer, cut up (or preferred parts to serve 4)
1 large onion, sliced thin
1/2 medium bell pepper, cut into small pieces
1 small (1-1/2 oz.) box raisins
1 cup raw rice*
1 cup water*
Salt and pepper
2 TBLS. butter or margarine
5 small pats of butter

*Since we love rice, we up both rice and water to 1-1/2 cups
Soak raisins in water to soften. Skin chicken (optional). In iron
skillet, saute chicken pieces in oil till golden. Remove to paper
towels and salt lightly. Pour off excess oil (about half). In
remaining oil, cook onion till golden. Add bell pepper and stir
and cook a minute. Then add rice and stir around and cook a
minute or two. Add water (or chicken stock), drained raisins,
salt, pepper and butter and stir and cook a minute or two.
Transfer rice mixture to buttered shallow baking dish. Arrange
chicken on top. Put pats of butter in corners and in center.
Cover with foil and bake in 350 degree oven for one hour.
Serves 4.

LEMON CHICKEN
FROM: Barbara Zuber

8 skinless, boneless chicken breasts
1/2 cup cornstarch
1/2 tsp. salt
1/8 tsp. red pepper
1/4 cup water
4 egg yolks, slightly beaten*
3 cups peanut or vegetable oil
4 green onions, sliced
Lemon sauce:
1-1/2 cups water
1/2 cup lemon juice (4 lemons)
3-1/2 TBLS. packed light brown sugar**
3 TBLS. cornstarch
3 TBLS. honey
2 tsps. instant chicken bouillon granules
1 tsp. grated ginger root

Pound breasts lightly to flatten. Combine cornstarch, salt and pepper in small bowl. Gradually blend in water and egg yolks. Pour oil into wok. Heat over high heat until oil reaches 375 degrees. Dip chicken breasts one at a time into cornstarch-egg yolk mixture. Fry breasts, 2 or 3 at a time, adjusting heat if necessary, until golden, about 5 minutes. Drain breasts on paper towels. Keep warm while cooking rest of chicken. Cut each breast into 3 or 4 pieces and arrange on serving plate. Sprinkle with sliced green onions. For sauce, combine all ingredients in medium saucepan. Stir until blended. Cook over medium heat, stirring constantly, until sauce boils and thickens, about 5 minutes. Pour over chicken. 6 to 8 servings.

*We use the leftover egg whites to make meringues.
**Tastes just as good with dark brown sugar. It just darkens the sauce.

ITALIAN SAUSAGE
FROM: Mrs. Joanna Litrico

Approx. 10-1/2 lbs. lean pork roast shoulder (Boston Butt cut good because it has little bone)
3/4 cup water
4-1/2 TBLS. salt
1-1/2 TBLS. freshly ground black pepper
1 TBL. anise seed*
1 scant TBL. light fennel seed*
1/2 tsp. crushed red pepper
Sausage casing (Refrigerated and stored between uses in a sealed jar of salt brine)

Cut pork into 2 inch cubes, trimming off largest chunks of solid fat. Put through meat grinder in a coarse grind. Add at intervals the water, salt, pepper, anise seed and light fennel seed as you mix continuously and thoroughly by hand. (Cleanse hands by wiping off with salt.) Remove cutting wheel from grinder and insert stuffing funnel. Blow into casing to open it up. (Sometimes may prepare under faucet to let water open up casing.) Mount casing on funnel very carefully to avoid tearing. Use needle to prick casing at beginning to prevent air voids. Put ground pork into casing by feeding it through grinder and funnel. Watch for air bubbles and prick with needle when necessary. Wipe down outside of stuffed casing with clean damp cloth. Tie a knot at start of casing to anchor the twine. Thread into links about 2-1/2" inches long with continous twine. (Technique is similar to a half-hitch or button-hole stitch. Holding sausage in left hand, carry ball of twine over sausage and then on the near side go between twine and sausage to form a loop. Pull loop tight at desired length, about 2-1/2 inches.) Continue linking to end and tie anchor knot. Rinse out wiping cloth well and wipe down outside casing again. Before refrigerating, allow sausage to air dry several hours by hanging it in loops over a clean rod. (Can use mop handle covered with foil suspended between 2 chairs.) In a warm house, air drying takes about 3 hours. In a cold room in wintertime, it can air dry overnight. Then put sausage in an open pan in refrigerator for a day or two before wrapping and freezing or wrapping to keep in refrigerator.

To cook, can skillet fry but preferred method is to roast - broil in oven. Prick several holes with fork in each link on both sides. Line bottom of broiler pan with heavy duty foil and place links on broiler rack. Roast in a 325 degree oven about 30 minutes, pricking more if air bubbles occur. Then turn oven to broil and brown one side. Turn and brown other side.

Recipe makes 13-1/2 feet of sausage, about 28 - 30 servings of two links each.

*Can use all fennel seed; no anise seed.

BEEF TENDERLOIN MARINADE
FROM: Phyllis Stoddard

For one tenderloin of beef:
1 cup sherry
1/2 cup cooking oil
2 or 3 cloves garlic
Ginger
Lawry's Lemon-Pepper
Cracked pepper
1/2 to 3/4 cup teriyaki sauce

Marinate for two days. Cook on grill. Best served rare.

STEAK ITALIAN
FROM: Rosa Finau

Bread crumbs, unseasoned
Grated Romano
Minced parsley
Minced garlic
Salt & pepper
Sirloin steak
Olive Oil or Mazola
Tomato Sauce
Mozzarella cheese

Make a breading of first 5 ingredients. Cut sirloin into serving pieces. (If thick, cut horizontally.) Dip in oil, then in breading. Place in greased baking dish. Pour tomato sauce over. Cook in a 350 degree oven to desired doneness. Add strips of mozzarella and broil until cheese melts.

POLYNESIAN TOMATO BEEF
FROM: Lola Mularkey

Mazola or olive oil
3 cloves garlic, chopped fine
2 lbs. flank steak or London broil, trimmed
1/3 cup soy sauce*
1/2 tsp. powdered ginger
1 large green pepper
1 can chop suey or chow mein vegetables, drained
1 can mushrooms, drained (or sliced fresh)
2 tomatoes, quartered
2 TBLS. cornstarch
1/4 cup water
2 cups rice
4 cups water
1/2 pkg. frozen peas

Saute chopped garlic in oil. Cut meat on bias as thin as possible (easier if you slightly freeze it first). Lay thin strips of meat on top of garlic and cook for just long enough to get the red out - not browned. Pour in soy sauce and add ginger. Simmer about 10 minutes. Cut pepper into strips and add to meat. Add drained Chinese vegetables and mushrooms. Put lid on and simmer 10 minutes until pepper is soft. Arrange tomato quarters around edges of pot and cook until slightly soft. Dissolve cornstarch in 1/4 cup of water and add to thicken sauce. Cook rice separately, putting in frozen green peas and letting them steam. Serve beef tomato dish over rice with tossed salad and garlic bread. Serves 8.
*Original recipe called for 1/2 cup.

REVVED UP ROAST BEEF
FROM: Pat Lee

Make small gashes in roast and insert slivers of garlic. Sprinkle Lea & Perrin's Worcestershire sauce liberally over it. Preheat oven to 500 degrees. Roast uncovered 7 minutes to the pound for rare, 10 minutes to the pound for well-done. Leave in oven for one hour without opening door.

ITALIAN FLANK STEAK
FROM: Sis Martin

1 to 1-1/4 lb. flank steak, pounded thin
1 hard boiled egg
2 garlic cloves
Handful of parsley
3 TBLS. olive oil
2 cloves garlic
Ragu*

In food processor, chop garlic cloves fine. Add parsley and chop fine. Add egg and chop fine. Spread mixture on steak, leaving a half inch clear at the edge all the way around. Sprinkle pepper over. Roll up steak and tie with string in 2 or 3 places. In skillet, heat olive oil and lightly brown garlic in it. Remove garlic. Brown rolled flank steak on all sides in oil. Pour ragu over. Put on low heat and cover. Cook for an hour, turning occasionally and basting with ragu. (Can cook in oven after browning, if desired.) Slice on the diagonal. Serves 4.

*The commercial ragus are fine, but ours is easy if you have the time. Our recipe is at the start of the pasta section. It makes twice the quantity needed for steak recipe above but freezes well for later use.

BARBEQUED RIBS AND CHICKEN
FROM: Gino and Helen Litrico

Everglades Seasoning*
10-12 lbs. ribs
2-3 chickens, quartered

Marinade:
2 8-oz. cans tomato sauce
1 cup olive oil or vegetable oil
1 cup orange juice
1/2 cup vinegar
3 tsps. dried oregano
2 pinches sweet basil
2 bay leaves, broken
2 tsps. salt
10-12 peppercorns
2 cloves garlic, minced

Glaze:
1/4 cup honey
1/2 tsp. dry mustard
1/4 tsp. ginger

At least 30 minutes before marinating (the longer the better), sprinkle meat liberally with Everglades Seasoning. In a large jar with a top, combine marinade ingredients and shake well. Marinate ribs and chickens in a shallow dish at room temperature one or two hours. We prefer to barbeque in our water smoker with a rib rack to cook a large quantity with no basting, turning or watching. Soon after lighting the charcoal, we put in the pan of water to get heated. When coals are evenly ash-gray, we toss in bay and hickory chips or sticks and put on the meat, well-coated with marinade. We cook one hour per pound according to the largest piece of meat. (We've used the same recipe on a grill, with ash-gray coals, basting as we turn the meat, allowing about an hour for chicken and a little longer for ribs.) When meat is done, brush with honey-mustard-ginger as a tasty glaze.

Everglades Seasoning also tenderizes, as it has papane (papaya) in it. It's distributed by Labelle Trading Post in Labelle, Florida, and is available at Publix.

INDIAN SPICED LAMB
FROM: Helen and Gino Litrico

Lamb shoulder chops have proved so economical and delicious when grilled that we've developed several recipes. This one uses the identical spices as the Indian corn recipe except for omitting the 2 tsps. salt.

Combine the following:
3 tsps. ground cumin
3 tsps. ground coriander
1 tsp. curry powder
1 tsp. chili powder
Dash turmeric, marjoram and cayenne

MIx spices well and rub into the chops, saving any excess in a sealed jar for next time. Let chops sit 20 or 30 minutes. Prepare a marinade of equal parts red wine and olive oil with just a touch of jalapeno sauce. Let marinate 20 minutes or more. Grill (or broil), season with salt and enjoy.
(The original spice mix for corn , when blended with melted butter, is delicious as a dip for grilled shrimp and even drizzled over walnuts or pecans as you roast them in the oven.)

BAKED PORK CHOPS
FROM: Juanita Gear

6 centercut 3/4" pork chops
1 cup rice
1-1/4 cups water
Salt & pepper
1 bell pepper, cut in rings
1 small onion, cut in thin slices
6 canned whole tomatoes, drained
1 cup water, or juice drained from tomatoes

Brown chops. Remove. Stir and brown rice in chop drippings. Add water and stir. Add salt and pepper and stir. Transfer to greased flat casserole. Arrange chops on rice. Top each with pepper ring, onion slice and drained tomato. Pour water or juice from tomatoes around on rice. Cover. Bake at 350 degrees for one hour. Serves 4 to 6.

PORK ROAST PINAY
FROM: Mrs. Phyllis Maines

1 large green pepper, seeded and cut in thin strips
2 or 3 cloves garlic, cut in slivers
1 boneless pork loin roast (about 3 lbs.)
1/4 cup water
1/2 cup dry white wine or dry Vermouth
1/3 cup white wine vinegar
1 tsp. salt
1 tsp. sugar
1/4 tsp. pepper
2 TBLS. soy sauce
1/8 tsp. ground ginger

Line bottom of heavy Dutch oven with green pepper strips.
Insert garlic slivers into meat. Combine 8 ingredients; pour over
meat. Roast uncovered in a 400 degree oven for 20 minutes.
Lower temperature to 350 degrees and continue roasting about
1-1/2 hours or until meat thermometer reaches 175 degrees.
Baste about every 25 minutes. Remove to serving platter. Skim
fat from pan juices and pass in bowl to serve over meat and rice.

STEAK LITRICO
FROM: Gino Litrico

Steak (sirloin, filet, ribeye or porterhouse)
Olive oil
Garlic powder
Oregano
Rosemary
Black pepper
OPTIONAL:
 Adolph's tenderizer, red wine, 1/2 tsp. jalapeno sauce

Trim off fat. Rub olive oil or good vegetable oil into steak on
both sides to prevent charring. Lightly sprinkle on both sides
garlic powder, oregano, black pepper, dried rosemary (crushed
between your fingers) and optional seasonings. Rub
seasonings into oiled steak. Let marinate about an hour before
grilling. Grill until desired doneness. Salt when serving.

MOIST MEAT LOAF
FROM: Helen Litrico

3/4 cup cheese crackers
Milk to cover
1 lb. ground chuck
1 small grated onion
1 egg, beaten
1 tsp. salt
1/4 tsp. pepper
1/4 tsp. ground nutmeg
1 cup catsup
2 TBLS. brown sugar
1/4 tsp. dry mustard
1/4 tsp. ground nutmeg

Crumble cheese crackers in small bowl, cover with milk and set aside. Combine next 6 ingredients and blend. Add soaked crackers to mix. Blend and put into buttered glass loaf pan in a 350 degree oven. After 40 minutes, cover with sauce made from last 4 ingredients. Cook 20 minutes more. Serves 6 and freezes well.

SICILIAN SURF 'N TURF
FROM: Victor Albanese

Saute small bits of squid in butter and onions and serve over steak as you normally would do mushrooms.

Vegetables

DERBY PARTY ASPARAGUS
FROM: Marie White

3 to 4 lbs. fresh asparagus
1 can heart of palm, sliced
1 large red pepper
1 large yellow pepper
Large pitted black olives, sliced

Clean and peel asparagus and steam no longer than 5 minutes
per bunch. Add sliced heart of palm and black olives. Cut
peppers in chunks a little smaller than a quarter. Pour
vinaigrette (see below) over all and marinate in refrigerator
overnight or several hours.

ANDRE'S VINAIGRETTE
FROM: Andre Perez

1/2 cup wine vinegar
2 TBLS. Dijon mustard
1/2 tsp. fresh or dry parsley and basil
Salt and pepper
Pinch of sugar
4 pieces garlic (minced)*
1/2 cup vegetable oil
1/4 cup virgin olive oil
Juice of 1/2 lemon (optional)

Mix vinegar and mustard spices first. Then add oils and lemon
juice. Blend well. *Can substitute garlic powder.

VEGETABLE QUICKIES
FROM: Eleanor Thornton

Green Beans - Steam very small green beans until crisp tender.
Rub with butter. Sprinkle with Mrs. Dash. Good hot or cold.

Zucchini Squash - Boil whole until crisp tender. Cut in half
lengthwise. Sprinkle with bouillion bits, butter, oregano and
grated Parmesan cheese. Broil briefly in toaster oven.

KAREN'S MARINATED GREEK VEGETABLES
FROM: Karen Weihs

Marinade:
1 cup white wine
1 cup lemon juice
1 cup olive oil
3 cups chicken broth
10 peppercorns or ground red pepper
1 clove garlic
1 tsp. thyme
1 tsp. dill
1 tsp. salt

Cook marinade for 45 minutes to blend all spices. Cut vegetables into bite-sized pieces and cook each separately - about 8 minutes as vegetables should be crisp. Steam green peppers and onion first. Spoon into another dish and set aside. Steam string beans and set aside. Steam zucchini and squash together. Cool and set in refrigerator with marinade spooned over. Keep overnight. Garnish with lemon wedges.

MOCK ARTICHOKES
FROM: Lynn Miller

3 cans French style green beans, drained and chopped fine
1/3 cup olive oil
3 large pods of garlic, minced
1 cup seasoned bread crumbs
1 cup grated Italian cheese
Little bit of salt and pepper

Reserve a little of bread crumbs and cheese for top. Mix well, top with crumbs and cheese, bake at 350 for 20-30 minutes.

MARINATED BROCCOLI
FROM: (Adapted from Charleston recipe)

Place raw broccoli flowerets in marinade of 2 parts oil, 1 part lemon juice, cayenne pepper, dry mustard and a little salt. Refrigerate. Drain.

NONNIE'S GREEN BEANS SICILIAN
FROM: Mrs. Joanna Litrico

Snap and wash green beans. Bring large pot of water to a rolling boil. (This retains the bright green color of the beans.) Add salt and then add beans. When water comes to second boil, lower heat to medium, cover and set timer at 10 minutes. When timer sounds, remove from heat immediately. Drain and leave in colander. To the empty pot, add about a quarter inch of oil and heat. Crack 2 or 3 cloves of garlic with the heel of your hand. Brown garlic in oil. Add beans. Drizzle a little vinegar around and add salt and pepper. Cover pot tightly and shake up and down real well so that all beans are well coated.

NONNIE'S ROASTED PEPPERS
FROM: Mrs. Joanna Litrico

4 large bell peppers
2 cloves garlic
1/2 TBL. salt
2 TBLS. oil

Put whole peppers on grill over hot coals. Turn until blackened evenly. Put into brown paper bag and seal tight so steam will loosen skins. After about 10 minutes, remove charred skin and all seeds and cut into large strips. Combine with garlic (broken up) and salt. Drizzle oil over top and stir. Remove garlic before serving, if desired.
OPTIONAL ADDITION - In iron skillet, put a one lb. can of tomatoes, mash and stir to cook lightly. Add one TBLS. oil, salt and pepper. Combine with bell pepper mixture.

NONNIE'S COLLARD GREENS SICILIAN
FROM: Mrs. Joanna Litrico

Fresh collards
Oil
3 or 4 cloves garlic
Half of 1 lb. can tomatoes
Salt & Pepper

Wash greens. Trim off stems and tough part of center rib. Fold each leaf into quarters and roll up like a fat cigar and cut into one-inch portions. Bring water to rolling boil, add salt and pile in the greens. (The hard boil helps preserve the color.) Boil until just tender, about 20 minutes - more if the greens aren't the freshest. Drain at once and leave in colander to drain dry. Cover bottom of cast iron skillet with about a quarter inch of good vegetable oil. Crack garlic with heel of your hand, add to hot oil and stir around until brown. Then add tomatoes and stir over medium heat until tomatoes almost dry out. Add drained collards to skillet, add a little salt and pepper. Stir around to mix flavors. (If it looks too dry, add a little water.) Remove from heat and serve.

PASTETTA
FROM: Mrs. Agata Rizzo

2 dozen blossoms of Zucchini, Squash, or Pumpkin
1 beaten egg
Little salt
1/3 cup milk
Almost 1 cup flour
Pepper (optional)
1/2 cup Mazola

Wash blossoms well and drain in colander until dry. Mix batter of egg, milk, flour, salt and pepper and blend until quite smooth. Heat oil in skillet. Holding blossom by stem end, dip in batter both sides until well covered. Fry in hot oil on both sides till lightly browned. Drain on paper towels. Eat immediately.

NONNIE'S FRITTATA
FROM: Mrs. Joanna Litrico

This recipe may be hazardous to your health. The first time Mrs. Litrico demonstated inverting the skillet to get the frittata out, this observer screamed,"What's to keep some oil from running down your arm and scalding you?" Her calm reply: "I say a little prayer."

Oil
3 large eggs beaten
2 TBLS. plain bread crumbs
2 TBLS. grated Romano cheese
1 clove garlic, minced fine
2 or 3 sprigs parsley, chopped fine
1 can drained asparagus or artichoke hearts
Salt & Pepper

Mix ingredients, adding asparagus or artichoke hearts last. In skillet, heat oil about a quarter inch deep until quite hot. Pour in mixture and shake pan to keep mixture loose. When bottom is set, put a plate over skillet to pour off oil. Invert frittata on plate. Put oil back into skillet and slide frittata back in to brown on other side. (Or you can use a Corning Ware skillet atop the stove and then remove the handle to run it under the broiler to brown other side without inverting.)

FRIED PEPPERS
FROM: Mrs. Joanna Litrico

In Catania, Sicily, they are deep-fried in oil over a brazier outside specialty shops and delicatessens for meats and cheese. Bought as a snack for theatre-goers, etc., along with ricotta fritters, anchovies, etc.

Trim off stems. Keep small peppers whole and keep seeds. Use generous amount of oil in skillet - about 1/2 inch deep. Fry in hot pot, turning often. Remove from oil and drain. Sprinkle with salt.

CABBAGE CASSEROLE
FROM: Mary Agnes White

1 small green cabbage
2 cups of light white sauce
1 cup grated sharp cheddar cheese
1/2 cup buttered bread crumbs

Make the white sauce: Melt one stick of Fleischman's margarine in small sauce pan. Add to melted margarine 1 tsp. salt, 1/2 tsp. black pepper and 2 TBLS. flour. Stir and cook together until flour taste is gone. Add 2 cups milk and cook, stirring constantly to keep from burning, until thickened. Put small amount of white sauce in 2-quart casserole. Cut up cabbage and place layer of cabbage on top of white sauce, add more white sauce, cheese and bread crumbs. Continue layering, ending with cheese and bread crumbs. Cook in 350 degree oven for 40 to 50 minutes. Serve immediately.

EGGPLANT CASSEROLE
FROM: Lola Mularkey

Peel eggplant. Slice in 1/2 inch slices and steam until soft. Mash up eggplant in bottom of casserole. Crumble 14 saltines on it. Then take a cup and add one egg and beat well, then add salt and fill cup with milk. Stir mix into eggplant. Dice good sharp cheddar cheese and dot all over. Bake in a 350 degree oven until it rises like a souffle - about 30 minutes.

ZUCCHINI WITH BLUE CHEESE
FROM: Mary Beth Grable

4 zucchini
2/3 cup mayonnaise
1 or preferably 2 TBLS. blue cheese
1/4 tsp. garlic salt
1/4 cup grated Parmesan cheese

Parboil zucchini. Drain. When cool enough to handle, halve horizontally. Combine next four ingredients and mix well. Spread over zucchini. Run under broiler for about 10 minutes until brown and bubbly.

STUFFED EGGPLANT SLICES
FROM: Mrs. Joanna Litrico

2 eggplants
Salt
Oil (to cover skillet 1/2" deep)
Meatball mixture*
1 lb. can of tomatoes
Grated Romano cheese

Remove part of skin from eggplant and slice 1/4" to 1/2" thick. Heavily salt both sides of each slice. Stack slices and press down. Allow to stand 30 minutes, press and occasionally squeeze over sink. In pan of water, wash off salt and squeeze slices to get out juice. Prepare meatball mixture to use half in this recipe. (Freeze other half or prepare as regular meatballs.) In iron skillet, heat oil and fry eggplant slices on one side only. Drain on platter until frying is completed. Then, wetting hands in dish of water to avoid stickiness, shape meat mixture into flat patty 1/2" thick to fit size of eggplant slices. In sandwich style, put meat between fried sides of slices and return to skillet. Fry until lower outside browns, then turn and brown other side. Remove from skillet and set aside. Drain off excess oil in skillet. Break up tomatoes and stir around, cooking a minute or two. In flat baking dish, put a layer (about 1/3) of tomatoes on bottom then layer (about 1/3) of eggplant-meat slices, then sprinkle a little grated Romano cheese. Repeat layers with cheese on top. Dot with few pats of butter. Cover. Cook in 350 degree oven about 15 minutes. Serves 4-6.

*Meatball mixture: Combine 1 lb. ground chuck, 1/3 cup plain bread crumbs, 3 sprigs cut up parsley, 1/4 cup finely grated Romano cheese, 2 beaten eggs, dash of salt and pepper and 1 TBL. of water or milk.

STEAMED SAUTEED VEGGIES
FROM: Helen Litrico

Steam cauliflower or broccoli flowerets (or combination) exactly five minutes. Drain. In skillet or wok, mix and warm 2 TBLS. olive oil, generous sprinkle of granulated garlic, a little lemon juice, salt and pepper. Add vegetables and saute briefly and serve.

121

CAPONATA
FROM: Mrs. Joanna Litrico

1 medium eggplant
Salt
1/2 cup olive oil
3 medium bell peppers, seeded and cut in strips
2 large onions, chopped
3 or 4 stalks celery, cut in chunks
1 one-lb. can tomatoes
1 clove garlic, minced
1/2 tsp. sugar
1 tsp. salt
Pepper to taste
1/4 cup stuffed green olives, cut in half
3 TBLS. capers
1 TBL. wine vinegar

Lengthwise, slice eggplant into about 6 or 8 slices. Salt each side heavily. Stack and press down. Let stand about 15 minutes. Squeeze down again. Wash off salt and pat dry with paper towels. Cut eggplant into half-inch cubes, unpeeled. In large skillet, heat half the oil. Add eggplant and cook gently while stirring, about 10 minutes. Remove eggplant. Add rest of oil and heat. Add onion, green pepper and celery and cook gently, stirring often, about 10 minutes. Add tomatoes, garlic, sugar, salt and pepper and cook 15 minutes longer. Stir in eggplant, olives, capers and vinegar. Cover and cook down over very low heat about 30 minutes. Serve cold or hot. Great with Italian bread.

CRISP YELLOW SQUASH
FROM: Mary Ellen Baker

Cut yellow squash in half horizontally and scoop out seeds. Combine chopped tomatoes and chopped onions with "too much" Parmesan, Lawry's Seasoned Salt, cracked black pepper and barely enough mayonnaise to hold together (about 1 tsp). Mix well and let sit. Then mound tomato mix in cavity of squash and sprinkle more Parmesan on top. Put a mere drop of oil on neck of squash to keep from scorching. Cook in a 350 degree oven about 20 minutes and serve immediately. (This should be crisp. Cook longer if you like less crunch.)

INDIAN CORN
FROM: Helen Litrico

16 ears of corn
3 tsps. ground cumin
3 tsps. ground coriander
2 tsps. salt
1 tsp. chili powder
1 tsp. curry powder
Dash of marjoram
Dash of turmeric
Dash of cayenne
1 stick butter, melted
2 limes cut into wedges

Shuck corn and cover with water in large pots and refrigerate at least an hour so moisture will penetrate cob. Combine next 8 ingredients and mix well. Mix about 1/3 of spicy mixture with melted butter in one service bowl. In second bowl, put dry spice mix with lime wedges. Cook corn directly on grill over medium coals, 4 or 5 ears at a time, and turn frequently until slightly browned all around. Eat this way: Dip pastry brush into butter-spice mix and brush up and down the ear. If you'd like more of the spicy taste, dip a lime wedge into the dry spices, then rub and squeeze spiced lime up and down the ear. Delicious but not for timid palates!

POTATOES AU GRATIN
FROM: Lynn Miller

1 24-oz. pkg. frozen Hash Browns, thawed
1 can cream of mushroom soup
1 can potato soup
2 cups sour cream
2 cups sharp cheddar cheese, grated
Little pepper (no salt necessary)

Mix well and put in greased pan. Bake in a 350 degree oven for 45 minutes.

ERMIE'S SCALLOPED POTATOES
FROM: Helen Litrico

8 all-purpose potatoes, peeled and cut in chunks
1/2 lb. sharp cheddar cheese, grated
2 TBLS. butter or margarine
Salt & Pepper to taste
2 eggs
1 cup milk (can or whole)

Parboil potatoes in salted water till tender. Drain well. In buttered casserole, put half of potatoes, half of cheese, second half potatoes, and rest of cheese. Mix eggs, salt, pepper, and butter in milk. Pour over potatoes and cheese and bake in 375 degree oven until cheese browns.

TATES AND ONIONS
FROM: Dr. Jim Baker

Potatoes, skins left on
Onion
Lawry's Seasoned Salt
Cracked Pepper
Oil

Slice potatoes (in rounds) and onions in a 50-50 proportion. Cover bottom of a Silverstone (or other non-stick) pan with oil. Place potatoes, onions, Seasoned Salt and pepper in pan and cook covered over medium heat to start and then lower heat. Turn vegetables over frequently. As mixture becomes dry, add water for moisture. Break up potatoes as they soften. Cook until potatoes and onions become mushy.

FRENCH FRIED MUSHROOMS
FROM: Mrs. Margaret Bird

Margaret got this recipe from a factory packaging mushrooms.

1 lb. fresh mushrooms
3/4 cup all-purpose flour
3/4 cup club soda
1/2 tsp. garlic salt

Wash mushrooms and dry thoroughly on paper towels. Small mushrooms may be left whole; cut large ones in 1/4 inch thick slices. Stir flour, club soda, and garlic salt together until smooth. Dip mushrooms in batter and fry in hot, deep fat 5 minutes or until golden brown.

TOMATO PIE
FROM: Nancy Duty

Make pie crust. Spread light coat of cream (or milk) on it. Bake in a 375 degree oven for about 5 minutes. Slice tomatoes fairly thin - enough to mound fairly high in crust. Combine 1/3 cup mayonnaise, 1/3 cup Parmesan cheese, 1 clove crushed garlic, pinch of sugar, salt and pepper. Mix with tomatoes. (Can add green pepper strips or sliced mushrooms.) Put tomato mix in crust and bake in a 350 degree oven about 30-40 minutes.

ANDRE'S RATATOUILLE
FROM: Andre Perez

Olive oil
Zucchini, sliced 1/2" thick
Onions, sliced and ringed
Green Peppers, cut in strips or rings
Tomatoes, cut in eighths
Salt & pepper
Parmesan cheese

Saute covered in a little bit of olive oil on low heat (Do onions and zucchini first). Add salt and pepper to taste. Add Parmesan cheese. Takes half an hour.

Salads & Slaw

LO-CAL CREAMY ITALIAN DRESSING
FROM: Helen Litrico

1/2 cup nonfat yogurt
1/2 cup mayonnaise
1/4 cup chopped parsley
1-1/2 tsps. lemon juice
1-1/2 tsps. Dijon-style mustard
1 clove garlic, finely chopped
1/4 tsp. oregano
1/8 tsp. black pepper

Combine in bowl and mix well. Store in sealed jar in refrigerator
Keeps a week or a little more.

FRENCH DRESSING
FROM: Bee Hendrickson

1/4 cup vinegar
Juice of one lemon
1/3 cup sugar
1 tsp. paprika
1/2 tsp. salt
1 crushed garlic clove
1/2 cup oil
1/3 cup catsup

Put first six ingredients in sealed jar and shake until sugar
dissolves. Add oil and catsup and shake well. Keeps well in
refrigerator.

STAY TRIM DRESSING
FROM: Pat Lee

This is one of the few low calorie dressings we really like. Use 1/3 cup with chunked tomatoes, cucumber and celery, adding parsley flakes, dillweed, rosemary and dried basil. Cover and refrigerate to blend flavors. Also good on a fresh spinach salad.

1 TBL. cornstarch
1/2 tsp. dry mustard
1 cup cold water
2 TBLS. vinegar
1/4 cup catsup
1/2 tsp. paprika
1/2 tsp. Worcestershire sauce
1/2 tsp. prepared horseradish
1/8 tsp. salt
1 small clove garlic, crushed

Combine cornstarch and mustard in a small saucepan; gradually stir in water. Place mixture over medium heat; cook, stirring constantly, until smooth and thickened. Cool. Add remaining ingredients; stir well. Pour dressing into an airtight container and chill. Shake well before using. Makes 1-1/3 cups - about 6 calories per serving, no cholesterol.

WONDERFUL POTATO SALAD
FROM: the late Agnes Olmsted

Cooked dressing:
3 TBLS. sugar
1 tsp. salt
1 tsp. dry mustard
1-1/2 TBLS. flour
1 egg
3/4 cup milk
1/4 cup cider vinegar
1 TBL. butter

Blend dry ingredients in top part of double boiler; add egg, then beat until smooth. Add milk, mix well. Place over boiling water; add vinegar a small amount at a time to avoid curdling. Stir constantly. Cook until thickened. Remove from heat, add butter. Cool thoroughly before using. Makes 1-1/4 cups.

Salad:
3 or 4 medium potatoes
1 cup chopped celery
2 TBLS. chopped onion
1 tsp. salt
1-1/2 tsps. sugar
1 or 2 TBLS. vinegar
2/3 cup cooked dressing

Scrub potatoes and cook in boiling water until just tender. Do not overcook. Cool slightly and peel them while they are warm. Cut into 3/4 inch cubes. Add celery and onion. Mix together remaining ingredients, including cooked dressing; pour over potatoes. Toss together lightly. Let stand at room temperature 10 minutes so potatoes can absorb the dressing. Cover and chill thoroughly. Makes 4 servings.

MARINATED OYSTER & PASTA SALAD
FROM: National Fisherman (Clare Vanderbeek)

This trade publication for the fishing industry consistently offers interesting recipes for seafood.

1 pint shucked oysters
1 cup Italian-style salad dressing
6 oz. (about 3 cups) spiral pasta, such as rotelle, uncooked
1/2 cup each red or green bell pepper strips, thinly sliced carrot,
      sliced mushrooms, thinly sliced celery, broccoli
      flowerets and thawed, frozen peas slightly cooked.
1/4 cup chopped parsley

Simmer oysters in their liquor over medium heat just until edges begin to curl, 3 to 5 minutes. Drain. Combine with salad dressing and refrigerate overnight. At least 2 hours before serving, cook pasta according to package directions. Drain oysters, reserving dressing. In large bowl, combine hot pasta with reserved dressing; let stand 15 minutes. Stir in oysters and vegetables. Refrigerate 2 to 12 hours. Makes 6 to 8 servings.

SHRIMP-RICE SALAD
FROM: Mrs. Lou Boshert

1 cup cooked rice
1 scant cup mayonnaise* (Thinned with 3 TBLS. lemon juice
and a dash Tabasco)
4 green onions, slivered
1/2 cup sliced stuffed olives
1 cup raw cauliflower, cut in bite size pieces
1/4 cup chopped green pepper
1-1/2 lbs. shrimp, boiled with usual seasonings

Mix vegetables first, add rice and mix, then mayonnaise. Mix. Refrigerate overnight. Toss and add cut-up shrimp before serving. (Best not to add shrimp the night before.)

*1-1/2 cups in original recipe

CURRIED CRAB-RICE SALAD
FROM: Karen Weihs

1 (7-1/2 oz.) can King Crab*
1 cup uncooked rice
1/4 cup salad oil
1 TBL. vinegar
1 tsp. salt
1/2 tsp. pepper
1/4 cup chopped pimiento
1/4 cup chopped parsley
1/4 cup chopped green onions
1/4 cup chopped green peppers
1/2 cup mayonnaise
2 TBLS. lemon juice
1 tsp. curry powder

Cook rice. Combine oil, vinegar, salt, pepper and toss with rice.
Cool. Add pimiento, parsley, onions, green pepper, and crab.
Toss. Combine mayonnaise, lemon juice, and curry powder.
MIx thoroughly into salad. Serve on greens. (Great as a
casserole too!) 8 servings.
        *For testing, we substituted a half pound of local fresh
crabmeat, and it was great both as a salad and a casserole.
Recipe should also be good substituting shrimp entirely or a half
and half combination of shrimp and crab.

BROCCOLI SALAD
FROM: Pat Lee

1 bunch fresh broccoli flowerets
1 cup raisins
1 small red onion or 3/4 medium one
2 TBLS. Hormel Bacon Bits
4 heaping TBLS. mayonnaise
2 TBLS. rice vinegar
1 scant tsp. sugar
Dash of hot sauce
1 can water chestnuts (optional)
        Combine broccoli and raisins. Slice red onion very thin
and separate into rings. Add bacon bits. Mix. Make dressing of
mayo, vinegar, sugar and hot sauce. Mix well and pour over
salad and mix. Refrigerate until serving time. Add sliced water
chestnuts if desired.

BROCCOLI SALAD
FROM: the late Juanita Lasserre

1 pkg. broccoli
3 hard cooked eggs, chopped
2 tsps. lemon juice
1-1/2 tsps. salt
4 tsps. Worcestershire
Dash Tabasco
2 env. plain gelatin
1 cup beef consomme
3/4 cup mayonnaise

Cook broccoli slightly until able to mash with fork. Mix with eggs, lemon juice, salt, Worcestershire and Tabasco. Soften gelatin in small amount of consomme. Add remaining consomme and heat until thoroughly dissolved. Cool. Combine consomme and broccoli mix and then add mayonnaise. Pour in mold and chill.

CAJUN FRUIT SALAD
FROM: Hon Versaggi

6 cups fresh fruit, cut up
1 can Eagle brand condensed milk

Mix well and chill. If any canned fruits are used, be sure to drain them first.

BLUEBERRY SALAD
FROM: the late Juanita Lasserre

2 3-oz. pkgs. blackberry gelatin
2 cups boiling water plus 1 cup juices and water
2-1/2 cups fresh blueberries, mashed
1 8-1/4 oz. can crushed pineapple
1 8-oz. pkg. cream cheese, softened
1/2 pint sour cream
1/2 tsp. vanilla
1/2 cup nuts

Dissolve gelatin in the 2 cups boiling water. Add the 3rd cup of liquid - the juices from drained pineapple and blueberries plus enough water to make 1 cup. Stir in the pineapple and the crushed berries. (If berries are a tough-skinned variety, cook a minute, just long enough to pop the skins.) Pour into 2-quart flat pan to firm up in refrigerator. Combine cream cheese, sour cream and vanilla and spread on congealed salad. Sprinkle with chopped nuts. Serves 10 or 12.

MANDARIN SALAD
FROM: Pat Lee

1 3-oz. pkg. orange Jello
3/4 cup hot water
Small carton cottage cheese
Small container Cool Whip
1 can Mandarin oranges
1 apple, peeled and chopped

Bring Cool Whip almost to room temperature for easier spreading. Dissolve Jello in hot water. Drain oranges, reserving juice. Add enough cold water to juice to make 3/4 cup. Combine Jello and juice mixes and blend in cottage cheese and Cool Whip. Let gel slightly before adding fruit. Refrigerate. Serves 8.

APRICOT SALAD
FROM: Mary Beth Grable

Mary Beth thinks her mother found this recipe in Southern Living 10 or 12 years ago. Nuts and dressing are optional.

2 (6-oz.) pkgs. dried apricots
3/4 cup water*
1/2 cup sugar
3 (3-oz.) pkgs. lemon-flavored gelatin
5 cups boiling water
1 (20-oz.) can crushed pineapple, drained
1 cup slivered almonds
Dressing

Combine apricots and 3/4 cup water in a saucepan; simmer until tender. Remove from heat and stir in sugar. Mash with a fork until smooth and set aside 1/2 cup for dressing. Dissolve gelatin in boiling water. Stir in remaining apricot mixture, pineapple and almonds. Pour into a 13 by 9 inch (no smaller) pan. Chill until firm. Cut into squares and top with dressing before serving. 15 generous servings, can easily stretch to 20 or even 24.

*We added a quarter cup of water while cooking.

Dressing for Apricot Salad

1 (8-oz.) pkg. cream cheese, softened
1/2 cup reserved mashed apricots
2 TBLS. sherry
1/2 pint whipping cream, divided
1/4 cup powdered sugar
1/2 tsp. vanilla extract
1/2 tsp. almond extract

Combine cream cheese, apricots, sherry and 4 tablespoons cream; beat until smooth. Whip remaining cream, add powdered sugar and flavorings. Fold into cream cheese mixture.
Yield: about 2-1/2 cups.

CLIFTON'S COLESLAW
FROM: The Florida Times-Union

This recipe comes from a cafeteria chain in Los Angeles.

3/4 lb. shredded cabbage (half a medium cabbage)
2 TBLS. sugar
1/2 tsp. salt
1/2 cup mayonnaise
1-1/2 TBLS. cider vinegar
Sprinkling of celery seed (editor's addition)

Toss cabbage, sugar and salt well and let sit for 10 minutes to weep. Do not drain. Combine mayonnaise and vinegar and toss with cabbage along with celery seed.

MILLER'S COLESLAW
FROM: Alec Miller

All ingredients are chopped very fine:
1/2 head of cabbage
2 medium tomatoes, unpeeled
1/2 bell pepper
1/2 medium onion (optional)
2 stalks celery
Generous sprinkling of celery seed
Dressing:
   4/5 cup mayonnaise
   1/5 cup vinegar
   Salt and pepper to taste

NON-SWEET SLAW
FROM: Eleanor Thornton

Cabbage, sliced thin
Kosher dill pickle
Minced onion and celery

Mix. Pour on a little juice from dill pickle. Mix gently by hand. Pour off excess. Add mayonnaise and mix. Prepare at last minute or it wilts.

135

Bread

NONNIE'S ITALIAN BREAD & PIZZA
FROM: Mrs. Joanna Litrico

This recipe makes 4 or 5 loaves and 2 large pizza crusts.

10-1/2 cups Pillsbury all-purpose flour, not sifted
2 pkgs. dry yeast
3 cups warm water
1 cup + 2 TBLS. Crisco
1-1/2 TBLS. salt

About 10 minutes in advance, dissolve yeast in one cup warm (not boiling) water. Combine flour, salt and one cup Crisco and blend together by hand, rubbing between palms. Add yeast water, blend by hand again. Add other two cups warm water and blend by hand. Knead vigorously. Blend in additional two TBLS. Crisco and knead again. (If becomes sticky, add a handful of flour.) Keep kneading until smooth. Place in slightly warmed pan and cover with warmed cheese cloths or clean dish towels and cover all with a warm wool sweater. Put in warm place. Allow to rise two hours or until doubled. Knead again. Allow to rise second time until doubled. Knead down for the third time. Divide into roughly seven parts. (If making pizza, the two parts for crusts are a little smaller than the five parts for loaves.) On floured surface, roll out dough by hand and shape into loaf, making 3 or 4 deep cuts with knife in each loaf. Put into ungreased baking pans curved into a crescent shape. Let rise third time about 2 hours. Put loaves into a 375 degree oven until done, about one hour. Toward end, can remove from pans and place directly on oven rack to get bottoms nicely brown.

PIZZA

After dough has risen twice (not 3 times as in bread), divide portion for pizza in half. Partially roll out with rolling pin on floured surface. Dot each pizza pan with teaspoon of oil and spread over surface. Then transfer dough to pizza tin and spread out to edge by hand. Prick with fork. Proceed with filling:

2 medium onions, sliced
2 small cans mushrooms, drained
1/3 cup oil

One 1 lb.-12 oz. can tomatoes
Salt & pepper
Salami or pepperoni, sliced thin (about half of an 8 oz. pkg.)
Mozzarella cheese - One 6 oz. pkg. sliced and one 4 oz. pkg.
        grated. Can substitute Provolone cheese.
Romano cheese - 2 TBLS. grated
1/2 tsp. oregano
1 minced garlic clove (optional)
Salt and fresh ground black pepper

Cook onions and mushrooms slowly in oil until lightly browned.
Add tomatoes, mash with fork, add salt and pepper to taste.
Cook slowly about 30 minutes. On prepared pizza dough,
distribute strips of mozzarella and salami. Pour tomato-onion
sauce over evenly. Sprinkle oregano generously over all (plus
optional minced garlic). Sprinkle salt and fresh ground black
pepper. Spread grated mozzarella and romano on top (about 1
TBL. grated romano on each pizza). Sometimes spread a little
more oil on top, if needed. Put in pre-heated 400 degree oven
for 30 minutes or more. (Ease up crust with spatula to see if
bottom is cooked). Serve hot. Freezes fairly well.

YOGURT BREAD

FROM: Phyllis Maines

2 cups warm water
1-1/2 TBLS. dry yeast
2 TBLS. honey or molasses
1 TBL. salt
1 cup plain yogurt
7-1/2 cups all purpose flour
1 egg white, beaten

Dissolve yeast in water. Combine ingredients except egg white.
No need to let rise in bulk. Knead, cut in half and knead again.
Shape into 2 loaves and place on pan on which you have
sprinkled a little corn meal or flour to prevent sticking. Make
slashes on top and cover. Let rise. Preheat oven to 350
degrees. Brush loaves with beaten egg white. Bake on upper
rack with steam pan of water on lower rack. Start checking at
30 minutes. Thump. If it sounds hollow, bread is done. (Like
thumping watermelons.) May take as long as 40 minutes,
depending on your oven.

HUSHPUPPIES
FROM: the late Jane Burbank

Jane Burbank's hushpuppies were a legend in her lifetime. She'd cook as many as 2,000 a night when the shrimpers had a big social. Like all great cooks, she never measured her liquids or seasonings, so these measurements are estimated here. Try this for an incredibly light hushpuppy.

2 cups self-rising corn meal
1 cup self-rising flour
1/2 cup pancake mix
Pinch salt
1 tsp. sugar
2 eggs
Enough milk to make real dough-y (about 1 cup)
Then add water (scant 1/2 cup)
1 large grated onion

Stir well. Let rest. Drop by teaspoonfuls into hot oil.

1878 GARLIC BREAD
FROM: Gene Oviatt

Make a mixture of Parmesan cheese, paprika, chopped parsley and green onion tops. Brush garlic butter on bread. Sprinkle mixture over. Cook in hot oven or under broiler.

SUNSHINE MUFFINS
FROM: Paula Margiotta

If running short of time, substitute a 6 oz. package of Mariani Tropical Medley (found in health food section of grocery store) for the papaya, pineapple, apricots, raisins and coconut, but use a large cooking apple instead of a medium one.

1-1/4 cups all purpose flour
1-1/4 cups sugar
1/2 tsp. baking powder
1/2 tsp. baking soda
1/4 tsp. salt
1-1/2 tsps. cinnamon
1 medium apple, grated
1/2 cup grated carrots
1/2 cup chopped pecans
1/2 cup chopped, dried papaya
1/2 cup chopped, dried pineapple
1/2 cup chopped, dried apricots
1/4 cup raisins
1/4 cup shredded coconut
2 large eggs
1/2 cup oil
1-1/2 tsps. vanilla

Combine dry ingredients, then add fruit, nuts and coconut. Mix the oil, eggs and vanilla and add to the above mixture. Spoon into a greased muffin pan. Bake at 350 degrees for 25 minutes. Makes one dozen.

BRAN FLAKE MUFFINS WITH BLUEBERRIES
FROM: Cynthia Parks

Substitute raisins when blueberries are not in season.

3/4 cup sifted flour (use part whole wheat if on hand)
2 1/2 tsps. baking powder
1/4 tsp. salt
2 TBLS. sugar
1 egg
3/4 cup milk
3 TBLS. salad oil
1 cup bran flakes
1 scant cup of blueberries

Sift dry ingredients together. Add others and stir. Pour into oiled 12-muffin tin and bake about 20 minutes at 400 degrees. (She mixes dry things in one bowl, egg, milk and oil in another and refrigerates overnight for a short-order special at breakfast.)

BUTTERMILK BISCUITS
FROM: Helen Litrico

The ingredient list is straight out of Mrs. S. R. Dull's Southern Cooking published in 1928. I re-wrote the directions, adding oven temperature and baking time - details she took for granted that every Southern lady knew.

2 cups flour (2-1/2 after sifting)
1 tsp. salt
1/2 tsp. soda
4 TBLS. shortening (Crisco)
1 cup buttermilk

Preheat oven to 450 degrees. Sift dry ingredients together. Cut in Crisco with two knives or pastry blender until the texture of coarse corn meal. Add buttermilk and mix with a fork to form a dough. Put a little flour on hands and lift onto a lightly floured board and knead only enough to make smooth. Roll or pat out to half inch thickness. Cut with biscuit cutter or fruit juice glass dipped in flour. Put on ungreased baking sheet and bake for 12 minutes.

BISCUITS
FROM: Helen Litrico

While the traditional Southern recipe (2 cups flour, 4 tsps. baking powder, 1 tsp. salt, 4 TBLS. Crisco, 1 cup sweet milk) is good and dependable, I've always had better luck with the variation below. Incidentally, I measure the Crisco by filling a 2 cup measuring cup with 1-2/3 cups water, then dropping spoonfuls of Crisco until the water level rises to 2 cups. Then drain off the water. This little extra moisture may make the difference.

2 cups sifted all-purpose flour
3 tsps. baking powder
1/2 tsp. salt
1/3 cup Crisco
3/4 to 1 cup milk

Preheat oven to 450 degrees. Sift flour, then measure. Then sift again with baking powder and salt. Cut Crisco into dry ingredients with two knives or a pastry blender until mixture looks like coarse corn meal. Pour in smallest amount of milk first and stir with fork until dough is mixed but rough-looking. Add remaining milk if necessary. Pat dough on a lightly floured board about 1/2 inch thick. The less flour you work into biscuits at this point, the lighter your biscuits will be. Cut dough with a biscuit cutter or fruit juice glass that has been dipped in flour. Bake on an ungreased cookie sheet for 12 to 15 minutes.

YOGURT CORNBREAD
FROM: Helen Litrico (Adapted from Nora Mill)

1 cup self-rising corn meal
1/2 cup olive oil
1/2 tsp. salt
2 eggs, beaten
1 cup no-fat yogurt
1/2 cup cream style corn

Combine corn meal and oil, add eggs and stir. Add remaining ingredients and mix. Put a buttered shallow baking dish in a 400 degree oven. When dish is hot, pour in mixture and bake 25 to 30 minutes.

VIRGINIA SPOON BREAD
FROM: Beth Tartan

2 cups boiling water
1 tsp. salt
3/4 cup yellow corn meal
3 TBLS. butter
2 eggs, separated
2/3 cup evaporated milk (a small can)
1 tsp. baking powder

Add corn meal to briskly boiling, salted water. Boil until just
thickened, stirring frequently. Add butter. Beat egg yollks, add
milk and stir into corn meal. Fold in stiffly beaten egg whites
and baking powder. Turn into buttered baking dish. Bake in
moderate oven, 375 degrees, about 40 minutes. Serves 6 to 8.

TOUGH BREAD
FROM: Helen Litrico

*This simple recipe handed down in my family is said to be
similar to a Swedish bread, only theirs has sugar in it (dough
would have to rise twice) and it is served sprinkled with
confectioner's sugar. The Italians also have a similar fried
bread.*

Roll dough
Hot cooking oil

Prepare your own hot roll recipe or use mix. After it has risen
once, grease your hands with butter and tear off bits of dough
about the size of a half-dollar. Stretch out dough gently (as you
do pizza) to form a patty thin enough to see through but no
holes. Have oil very hot and toss a number of these discs in.
They rise to surface when done and must be eaten at once or
you'll soon know how it got its name.

AMELIA MUD PIE
FROM: Chris Weihs

Shell:
Oreo cookies
2 TBLS. butter

Filling:
15 oz. Chocolate ice cream, softened
2 TBLS. ground coffee
2 TBLS. Sanka
2 TBLS. whipped cream
2 TBLS. brandy
2 TBLS. Kahlua

Topping:
Kraft fudge topping
Whipped cream
Cherry

Crush Oreo cookies very fine and mix with melted butter. Press into pie pan and place in freezer. Whip chocolate ice cream with ground coffee, Sanka, brandy and Kahlua. Fold in whipped cream and place in shell. Return to freezer until firm. Cover surface with Kraft fudge topping. When serving, top with whipped cream and a cherry.

TOFFEE BARS
FROM: Marie White

Line a large shallow baking pan with foil and spray with Pam. Cover with one layer of saltines, side-by-side. Boil 2 sticks butter and one cup brown sugar 4 to 6 minutes. Pour over crackers. Bake in a 375 degree oven for about 6 minutes (Watch for burning). Pour 12 oz. semi-sweet chocolate chips over all and return to oven until chocolate chips melt. Remove from oven. Spread chocolate chips around and cool. Chill in refrigerator overnight or at least 4 hours. Dump out of pan and break into pieces by hand or bring to room temperature and cut.

CHOCOLATE CREAM CHEESE CAKE
FROM: Better Homes & Gardens (Mrs. Jody Cate)

The frosting comes from part of the batter in this top scratch-cake winner.

2 3-oz. pkgs. cream cheese, softened
1/2 cup butter or margarine, softened
1 tsp. vanilla
6-1/2 cups (1-1/2 lbs.) sifted powdered sugar
1/3 cup milk, at room temperature
4 squares (4 ounces) unsweetened chocolate, melted & cooled
4 TBLS. butter or margaine, softened
3 eggs
2-1/4 cups all-purpose flour
1 tsp. baking powder
1 tsp. baking soda
1 tsp. salt
1-1/4 cups milk

Cream together cheese, the 1/2 cup butter or margarine, and the vanilla. Alternately beat in sugar and the 1/3 cup milk. Blend in chocolate. Remove 2 cups for frosting; cover and refrigerate. Cream together remaining chocolate mixture and butter. Add eggs; beat well. Stir together dry ingredients. Beat into creamed mixture alternately with the remaining milk. Turn into two greased and floured 9 x 1-1/2 inch cake pans. Bake in a 350 degree oven for 30 minutes. Cool in pans 10 minutes. Remove; cool on racks. Remove frosting from refrigerator 15 minutes before frosting cake.

ADA POWELL'S PEAR PIE
FROM: Sandra Wurtman

Cook 6 to 8 large pears, seasoned with butter and sugar, until tender. Remove 1 cup juice from pears and add 1/2 stick butter, 3/4 cup sugar, 2 TBLS. cornstarch, little lemon juice and cinnamon. Cook, then set sauce aside. Cook pie crust and cool. If pears are too juicy, add a little cornstarch before removing from stove. Put pears in pie crust and place strips of pie crust on top. Bake. When served, put sauce on top. Can be served hot or cold. Freezes well. Remove from freezer and warm through.

PERSIMMON PRALINE PIE
FROM: Adeline Davis

4 cups sliced persimmons
1 stick oleo
3/4 cup granulated sugar
1/2 cup firmly packed brown sugar
2 TBLS. quick cooking tapioca
1/2 cup chopped pecans
3 TBLS. lemon juice
1 cup biscuit mix

Mix persimmons, granulated sugar and tapioca in large bowl. Let stand while preparing rest. Combine biscuit mix and brown sugar in small bowl, cut in oleo with pastry blender until mixture is crumbly. Stir in pecans. Sprinkle one-third over bottom of a 9" pie plate, top with persimmon mixture. Sprinkle remaining pecan mixture on top. Bake in very hot oven (450 degrees) for 10 minutes. Lower to 350 degrees and bake 20 minutes longer or until topping is golden. Cool on wire rack before cutting. Serve warm or chilled.

FRESH APPLE CAKE
FROM: the late Margaret Allan

2 cups sugar
1-1/2 cups Wesson Oil
2 eggs
3 cups all-purpose flour
1 tsp. soda
1/4 tsp. cinnamon
3 fresh apples
1-1/2 cups nuts

Dice apples, sprinkle with one cup of the sugar and let stand for at least 30 minutes. Mix remaining cup of sugar with oil, eggs, flour, soda and cinnamon. Blend thoroughly. Add diced apples and chopped nuts last and blend. Put in greased tube pan and bake at 350 degrees about 1 hour and 15 minutes.

FIG CONSERVE
FROM: Sally Taleen

Use whole, unpeeled figs, keeping small stems. Cover each 2 cups figs with 1 cup sugar - no water. (Refrigerate overnight - optional.) Use heavy-bottom aluminum pot to keep sugar from sticking. Bring to low boil and keep cooking until juice is thick as honey - could be 1 or 1-1/2 hours or more. Stir occasionally, taking care not to break fruit. After first half hour of cooking, add sliced lemons (not too thin). About 15 minutes before anticipated finish, add pecan halves and raisins. Pack in sterilized jars, adjust lids and put in boiling water bath at 212 degrees for 10 minutes (pint jars).

PECAN DUMP CAKE
FROM: Nancy Duty

Large can of crushed pineapple
1 cup firmly packed dark brown sugar
1 pkg. yellow cake mix
1-1/2 sticks margarine
2 cups or more chopped pecans

Grease baking pan about 15" long. Pour in crushed pineapple. Over this, distribute the brown sugar. Cover with cake mix. Cut margarine into thin slices and spread over (or melt and pour over). Spread chopped pecans on top. Bake at 350 degrees for one hour.

LEMON PUFFS
FROM: Louise Mullis

1 box lemon cake mix
1 8-oz. carton Cool Whip
1 egg, beaten
Powdered sugar

Mix first 3 ingredients by hand. Drop by spoonfuls into hand and shape into ball. Roll in powdered sugar. Put on ungreased cookie sheet allowing room for cookie to flatten out. Bake in preheated 350 degree oven until lightly brown.

148

BROWNIES
FROM: Helen Litrico

1/2 cup butter or margarine (1 stick)
1 cup sugar
2 eggs
1/2 cup all-purpose flour, sifted
Few grains salt
1 cup pecans, chopped
2 squares (2 oz.) unsweetened chocolate
1/2 tsp. vanilla

Put chocolate on low heat to melt. Start oven at 350 degrees or
moderate. Grease a shallow oblong tin baking pan or 8" square
pan. Work butter or margarine until creamy and add sugar
gradually. Taking time here determines good results. Add
eggs, one at a time, beating hard after each addition. Sift in
flour and salt. Beat again. Mix in nuts, melted chocolate and
vanilla and pour into greased pan. Bake 25 to 30 minutes.
Tops should be soft when touched. Cool in pan, then cut into
squares.

LEMON BARS
FROM: Pat Couturier

Crust:
1 cup butter
2 cups flour
1/2 cup powdered sugar
Melt butter and mix above together. Press in 9 x 13 inch (be
sure of size!) greased and floured pan. Bake at 325 degrees for
20 minutes.
Filling:
4 eggs, well beaten
2 cups sugar
1/2 tsp. salt
7 TBLS. lemon juice
1 tsp. baking powder
4 TBLS. flour

Pour over hot cookie crust. Bake 30 minutes at 325 degrees.
Cool and sprinkle with powdered sugar. Cut into squares.

PECAN PIE
FROM: Helen Litrico

One 9" unbaked pie shell
1 cup sugar
1/4 cup (1/2 stick) butter, melted
2/3 cup dark or light corn syrup
1 TBL. all-purpose flour
1/4 tsp. salt
3 eggs, slightly beaten
1 tsp. vanilla
1 cup chopped pecans

Start oven at 450 to preheat. Combine sugar, butter, syrup and mix well. Stir in flour, salt and eggs. Add pecans and vanilla and mix. Pour into pie shell and bake in preheated 450 degree oven 10 minutes, then reduce to 325 degrees for another 25-30 minutes or until filling is almost firm in center. Cool. Serves 8.

LEMON CUSTARD PIE
FROM: Beth Tartan

Beth Tartan is the pen name of Elizabeth Sparks, food editor of the newspaper in my hometown of Winston-Salem, N. C.

2 cups sugar
2 TBLS. cornmeal
1 TBL. flour
4 eggs, unbeaten
1/4 cup melted butter
1/4 cup milk
1/4 cup lemon juice
4 tsps. grated lemon rind
Unbaked 9-inch pastry shell

Mix sugar, cornmeal and flour. Add eggs, one at a time, and beat well after each. Stir in butter, milk, lemon juice and rind. Mix well. Pour into the unbaked pastry shell. Place on rack near bottom of oven. Bake in a moderate oven, 350 degrees, 45 minutes or until done. Allow to cool before cutting.

MAMIE EISENHOWER'S FUDGE
FROM: The Florida Times-Union

4-1/2 cups sugar
2 TBLS. butter or margarine
Dash salt
1 (13-oz.) can evaporated milk
1 (12-oz.) pkg. semisweet chocolate pieces
3 (4-oz.) pkgs. sweet cooking chocolate, broken
2 cups marshmallow cream
2 cups chopped walnuts or pecans

Combine sugar, butter, salt and milk in a large saucepan. Bring to boil over medium heat, stirring constantly. Boil 6 minutes, stirring occasionally. Combine chocolates, marshmallow cream and nuts in mixing bowl. Pour syrup over chocolate and beat until chocolate is melted. Turn in well-greased 13 x 9 inch pan. Cool several hours or until firm. Cut into squares and store in airtight container. Yield: about 5 pounds.

COCONUT BON BONS
FROM: Barbara Chadwick

Filling:
2 boxes 10X sugar
1 14-oz. bag flaked coconut
1 stick margarine, melted
1 can sweetened condensed milk
1 cup pecans or almonds (optional)

Coating:
1 large package chocolate chips
1/2 cake parafin

Make filling: Mix sugar and coconut, then add margarine and milk. Add nuts, if desired. This is a very stiff mixture and best mixed by hands. Roll in small 1-inch balls. Set aside 2 hours to dry.
Make chocolate coating: Melt chips in double boiler over barely boiling water. Add parafin and let melt completely.
Dip coconut balls into chocolate with toothpick. Makes about 200 balls.

VODKA-KAHLUA CAKE
FROM: Marie White

1 box yellow cake mix
1 small pkg. instant chocolate pudding
4 eggs
1 cup salad oil
1/4 cup water
1 cup vodka
1/2 cup Kahlua

Mix everything in large bowl about 2 minutes. Grease or spray Bundt pan. Bake 50 minutes at 350 degrees. Cool completely. Glaze with mixture of 2 TBLS. melted butter and 1 cup powdered sugar, thinned with Kahlua. Cake will be very moist inside.

CARROT PIE
FROM: Alice Pitts

1 32-oz. pkg. of carrots
1/2 cup butter
1 cup sugar
1/2 cup canned cream
2 whole eggs
1/4 tsp. salt
1 tsp. nutmeg
1-1/2 tsps. cinnamon
1 tsp. allspice
1 tsp. vanilla

Peel, cut and boil carrots in salted water till tender. Drain and mash or whip. Then add sugar, butter, canned cream and mix. Beat and add eggs, then spices. Fills one 9-inch pie shell. Bake at 350 degrees for 50-55 minutes. Top with whipped cream.

BLUEBERRY CAKE
FROM: Mrs. Lynn Shad

Use one 9" by 13" pan or two standard brownie pans.

1/2 cup butter (1 stick)
2 cups sugar
2 eggs
3-1/4 cups all-purpose flour
1 tsp. cream of tartar
1/2 tsp. soda
1 cup milk
1 quart blueberries
1/2 cup sugar
1 tsp. cinnamon
1 stick butter, melted

Cream butter and sugar, beat in eggs. Alternate dry ingredients and milk, beating in well after each addition. Fold in berries. Put in well-greased baking pan (s). Sprinkle mixed sugar and cinnamon on top. Bake in a 350 degree oven for 50 minutes. After baking, brush with melted butter. Freezes well.

BLUEBERRY QUICK
FROM: Mrs. Lynn Shad

Melt 1 stick butter in flat baking pan in oven. Combine 1 cup flour, 1 cup sugar and 1 cup milk. Stir well and pour into pan over butter. Put 3 cups blueberries on top. Bake at 350 degrees for 45 minutes. Cool 20 minutes.

FRESH COCONUT CAKE
FROM: Flora & Ella's Labelle

Barbara Zuber found this jewel in a book entitled Famous Florida! Underground Gourmet Restaurants, Recipes and Reflections. She makes it in two 9" pans and uses a serrated knife to cut them into four layers. We like to hold out some of the coconut to fling on top for a nice raggedy look.

1 box cake mix (white, yellow or chocolate)
16 oz. coconut
16 oz. sour cream
2 cups sugar
9 oz. whipped topping (Cool Whip)

Prepare cake mix according to directions baking in 3 9" pans (it will take less time than directions say so watch carefully 10 minutes before end of baking time). Combine coconut, sour cream and sugar. Let stand 2 hours. After cake has cooled, place one layer on serving plate. Reserve one-half cup of coconut mixture for topping. Spread half of remainder on bottom layer. Place second layer on top and use remaining half of coconut mixture to cover. Mix the one-half cup reserved coconut mixture together with whipped topping. Frost top and sides of cake with it. Refrigerate for two days before serving. The wait is worth it!

SUSIE'S LEMON PIE
FROM: Mary Jane Sexton

Put in double boiler:
3 egg yolks
3/4 cup sugar
2 level TBLS. flour
lump butter

Add 1 cup boiling water, juice and grated rind of one lemon. Stir all until thick. Put in baked pie shell and top with meringue made of whites of 3 eggs. Beat and add one TBL. sugar at a time until you use 7-1/2 TBLS. sugar. Cook until brown in a 325 degree oven.

154

PUMPKIN MINCEMEAT PIE
FROM: Sara Severud

Pastry for 9" pie
2 cups mincemeat (Cross & Blackwell Mincemeat with rum & brandy)
1/2 cup brown sugar
1/2 tsp. salt
1/2 tsp. cinnamon
1/4 tsp. ginger
1/4 tsp. ground cloves
1 cup canned strained pumpkin
2 eggs
3/4 cup evaporated milk
Garnish: whipped cream and toasted almond slivers

Line 9" pie plate with pastry. Crimp the edge. Spread 2 cups mincemeat over the bottom. Bake in hot oven (425 degrees) for 15 minutes. While this bakes, mix together brown sugar, salt, cinnamon, ginger and ground cloves. Combine spice mixture with 1 cup canned strained pumpkin. Beat 2 eggs slightly and add to 3/4 cup evaporated milk. Mix thoroughly. (You can use pumpkin pie mix using directions on the can.) Take pie from oven and cool oven to 350 degrees. Ladle pumpkin mix gently over mincemeat. Bake in moderate oven until pumpkin custard is set (about 35 minutes). Serve with whipped cream and toasted almond slivers.

DIETER'S TRIFLE
FROM: Lynn Miller

This delightful dessert comes from Weight Watcher's.
1 angel food cake
2 pints sliced strawberries
2 cans chunk pineapple in natural juice, drained
4 sliced bananas
2 cans lite cherry pie filling
2 Kiwi fruit, sliced
Low-calorie Cool Whip
In trifle bowl or clear glass dish, break up cake with hands to cover bottom. Then arrange fruits and pie filling in layers. Repeat cake and fruit layers, reserving some strawberries and Kiwi slices. Cover with Cool Whip and garnish with strawberries and Kiwi slices.

OATMEAL DROPS
FROM: Phyllis Maines

1-3/4 cups sifted flour
1/2 tsp. baking soda
1 tsp. salt
1/2 tsp. cinnamon
1/4 tsp. ground cloves
3/4 cup shortening
1/2 cup sugar
1 cup brown sugar, packed
1 egg
1/2 cup buttermilk
1/4 cup light corn syrup
1 tsp. vanilla extract
2 cups quick-cooking oatmeal
1 cup chopped nuts
1 cup seedless raisins

Heat oven to 375 degrees. Sift together into a large bowl the flour, soda, salt, cinnamon and cloves. In another bowl, cream the shortening and gradually add the sugars, creaming well. Add the egg and blend well. Combine the buttermilk, corn syrup and vanilla extract. Add the dry and liquid ingredients to the sugar mixture, beginning and ending with the dry ingredients. Blend in the oatmeal, nuts and raisins.
For big cookies, drop by rounded tablespoons 2 inches apart onto greased cookie sheet. Bake at 375 for 12 to 15 minutes. Makes about 4-1/2 dozen.
For little cookies, drop by teaspoonfuls onto greased cookie sheet. Bake at 375 for 7 minutes. Makes 10 dozen.

AMARETTO CAKE
FROM: Connie Hogan

1 pkg. yellow cake mix without pudding
1 pkg. instant vanilla pudding (3-1/2 oz. size)
4 eggs
1/2 cup Amaretto
1/2 cup oil
1/3 cup finely chopped nuts, preferably almonds
Topping:
4 TBLS. butter or margarine
1/4 cup Amaretto
1/2 cup brown sugar

Grease and flour tube pan. Cover bottom with chopped nuts. Stir together dry cake and pudding mixes, then beat in eggs, oil, and Amaretto, just until smooth. Pour into pan over nuts and bake in a 300 degree oven 1 hour and 15 minutes or until done. (It is normal for cake to crack on top.) Remove from oven and let stand while you quickly prepare topping.
Topping:
Place ingredients in heavy small saucepan and bring to boil, stirring. Remove from heat and, with skewer or ice pick, poke holes in cake; spoon warm topping over hot cake. Spoon and poke till all is absorbed. Let cake cool in pan and then invert. Let sit overnight.

DELICATE LEMON PUDDING
FROM: Jane Keily

2 TBLS. butter
2/3 cup sugar
2 separated eggs
2 TBLS. lemon juice & rind
2 TBLS. flour
1 cup milk

Cream butter, add sugar. Beat egg yolks until thick and lemon colored. Add to creamed mixture with juice and rind. Fold in flour, stir in milk. Beat egg whites stiff. Fold into first mixture. Put in 1 or 1-1/2 quart greased dish set in pan of hot water in 375 degree oven for 35-40 minutes. Top turns brown so don't undercook.

FRUIT PIZZA
FROM: Helen Litrico

This came out of a cookbook published a few years ago by a civic organization in Jacksonville - the Symphony Guild, I believe.

1 pkg. (1 lb. 4-oz.) Pillsbury Sugar Cookie dough
1 8-oz. pkg. cream cheese, softened
2 TBLS. sugar
1 tsp. vanilla
Sliced fresh fruit of your choice - strawberries, grapes, peaches, kiwi fruit, bananas, etc. (If use canned fruit such as mandarin oranges, drain first and save juice for glaze.)
Apricot or peach preserves or marmalade

Slice cookie dough about 1/4 inch thick and layer all over the bottom of a large pizza pan. Bake in a 350 degree oven for 12 minutes. Cool. Mix together softened cream cheese, sugar and vanilla and spread over cookie crust. Then arrange fruits in circular fashion on top. Heat preserves with a little water or the juice from any canned fruit. Then spread as a glaze all over fruit. Refrigerate until serving.

BANANA BREAD
FROM: the late Louisa McGaughey

1/2 cup butter
1-1/2 cups all-purpose flour
1 cup brown sugar
1 tsp. soda
pinch of salt
1 cup nut meats
2 eggs
3 ripe bananas
1 tsp. baking powder

Cream butter, add sugar and eggs. Stir smooth and add crushed bananas. Sift flour and dry ingredients together. Add to first mixture and add nuts. Bake in a moderate oven for 50-60 minutes.

BROWNIE PUDDING
FROM: the late Jean Cavin

1 cup flour
2 tsps. baking powder
3/4 cup white sugar
1/2 tsp. salt
2 TBLS. cocoa
1/2 cup milk
1 tsp. vanilla
2 TBLS. melted shortening
3/4 cup chopped nuts
3/4 cup brown sugar
1/4 cup cocoa
1-1/2 cups hot water

Sift together flour, baking powder, salt, granulated sugar and cocoa. Add milk, vanilla and shortening. Mix well; add nuts. Pour into shallow baking dish. Mix brown sugar and cocoa, sprinkle over batter, then pour hot water over entire batter. Bake in moderate oven (350) for 40-45 minutes.

POUNDCAKE
FROM: The Florida Times-Union food pages

2 sticks margarine
1/2 cup vegetable shortening
3 cups sugar
4 eggs
1 cup milk
3 cups cake flour, unsifted
1 tsp. vanilla
1 tsp. almond extract

Cream margarine and shortening. Add sugar, cream together. Add eggs, one at a time, then milk, flour and flavoring. Set oven at 300 degrees. Do not preheat oven - start cake in cold oven. Bake approximately 1 hour to 1 hour and 15 minutes.
Glaze:
Mix together 1 cup powdered sugar and enough lemon juice to moisten. Glaze will be thick. Dribble over cake while cake is still warm.

APPLE CRISP PUDDING
FROM: Phyllis Maines

1 cup graham cracker crumbs
1 TBL. flour
1 cup chopped pecans and/or walnuts
1 cup light brown sugar
1/4 cup granulated sugar
1 TBL. grated orange rind
Dash of salt
1/2 tsp. cinnamon
1/2 tsp. nutmeg
1/2 cup melted butter
4 large tart apples, peeled, cored and thinly sliced
Lemon juice

Mix together graham cracker crumbs, flour, pecans and/or walnuts, brown sugar and granulated sugar. Season with orange rind, salt, cinnamon and nutmeg. Moisten with melted butter. Lightly butter a 9" x 9" x 2" baking dish and cover the bottom of the dish with a layer of apples. Scatter some of the crumb mixture over top and then sprinkle with lemon juice. Repeat, ending with a layer of the crumb mixture. Bake 45 minutes in a 350 degree oven. Serve warm with cream. Makes 6 servings.

LEMON FREEZE
FROM: Nan Sands

4 egg yolks, well beaten
2 cans Eagle Brand Milk
1 cup lemon juice (8 lemons)
1 tsp. lemon rind, grated
4 egg whites
6 TBLS. sugar

Beat egg yolks until thick and lemon colored. Add milk, lemon juice and rind and stir until thick. Beat whites till stiff and gradually add sugar. Fold whites into lemon mixture and pour into parfait glasses. Freeze till firm. If made the night before and frozen, set out to soften before serving. Serves 8.

INDEX

Baked Red Bass	87	Peppercorn Chicken	
Caper Sauce	90	Breasts	99
Clam Sauce for		Peppery Chicken	
Spaghetti	95	Breasts	100
Crabmeat Stuffing		Pollo con Rizzo e	
for Baked Fish	85	Uva Seca	105
Cucumber-Dill Sauce		Spanish Chicken	104
for Fish	92	Zia's Grilled Chicken	97
Dieter's Baked Fish	86		
First Course Oysters	93		
Fish Quiche	90	**Meats**	
Gravlax	83		
Grilled Curried Seafood	85		
Grilled or Broiled		Baked Pork Chops	112
Bluefish	86	Barbequed Ribs	
Herb Baked Grouper	89	and Chicken	111
Inland Paella	91	Beef Tenderloin	
Marinade for		Marinade	108
Grilled Fish	83	Indian Spiced Lamb	112
Oyster Fritters	95	Italian Flank Steak	110
Oyster Gravy	93	Italian Sausage	107
Oyster Pie	94	Moist Meat Loaf	114
Oyster Pilau	95	Polynesian	
Sauteed Fish Fillets	89	Tomato Beef	109
Sauteed Flounder	84	Pork Roast Pinay	113
Sauteed Trout	84	Revved Up Roast Beef	109
Savannah Kingfish	87	Sicilian Surf 'n Turf	114
Scalloped Oysters	94	Steak Italian	108
Shark Oriental	88	Steak Litrico	113
Simple Baked			
Fish Fillet	86	**Vegetables**	

		Andre's Ratatouille	125
Chicken		Andre's Vinaigrette	115
		Cabbage Casserole	120
Chicken Cacciatore	97	Caponata	122
Chicken Kiev		Crisp Yellow Squash	122
with Shrimp	102	Derby Party Asparagus	115
Chicken Marbella	103	Eggplant Casserole	120
Chicken Reuben	99	Ermie's Scalloped	
Chicken Rosemary	98	Potatoes	124
Lemon Chicken	106	French Fried	
Oven Barbequed		Mushrooms	125
Chicken	101	Fried Peppers	119

164